BLUEPRINT

BLUEPRINT

THE AGENT'S GUIDE TO BUILDING A THRIVING REAL ESTATE BUSINESS

GARRY CREATH
CHRIS SCOTT

LIONCREST
PUBLISHING

BLUEPRINT

The Agent's Guide to Building a Thriving Real Estate Business

ISBN   978-1-5445-0246-5 *Paperback*
       978-1-5445-0247-2 *Ebook*

This book is dedicated with the greatest love and respect to my wife and muse, Pamela. Her continuous support was instrumental in pushing me to complete this work, and she was the most caring proofreader and loving critic.

—GARRY CREATH

Nicole, Claire, Madeline, Maxwell, and Vincent. My Why.

—CHRIS SCOTT

We would like to further dedicate this book to all of the real estate brokers, agents, and team leaders who support us in our journey as we strive to bring the best tools, technologies, and resources to the industry. Thank you for being such loyal clients, and thank you for working every day to take exceptional care of your clients, build a better and sustainable business for yourself, and ultimately improve the real estate industry as a whole.

—GARRY & CHRIS

CONTENTS

INTRODUCTION

If you asked a room full of real estate agents what the most important part of their job was, seven out of ten would likely say something like "service." Two out of ten of those agents would probably say "sales" or "lead generation." And those two would likely be selling more properties than those focused on service.

But a lone agent would say something different: "business owner" or "entrepreneur."

That one agent would be focused on building something that rewards now but, more importantly, will continue to pay them long after they've stopped showing homes and putting signs in yards. That one agent would be focused on a blueprint that will help them build a business—they know they're not simply working another job.

Real estate professionals often overlook this key aspect of their role. Whether you're a solo operating agent, you're working out of a broker's office, or you're that broker or team leader running the office, you're absolutely an *entrepreneur*. As agents, we're all entrepreneurs and businesspeople. A real estate practice is a business you own rather than a job you attend.

Most real estate professionals feel comfortable providing a service. They are excellent at customer service for their buyers and sellers, and they've found one or two particular activities that they are comfortable doing as part of the process. They aren't as comfortable with sales and marketing, however. And they aren't at all comfortable with finances.

What they haven't yet recognized is that they've started a business—that they're entrepreneurs, and their success depends on more than just doing the aspects that they enjoy.

This isn't a surprise, really. According to the National Association of Realtors®, by the time we become real estate professionals, it's actually our second or third—or fourth or fifth—career. Life goes sideways, your nine-to-five job ends, and you get sold on the idea that real estate is an easy alternative.

Sales, marketing, and business finance classes aren't

required to get your real estate license. Realtors® are highly interpersonal—we love being around people and helping them, and we are "people persons" by nature. But we also need to learn business, sales, and financial savvy. Unfortunately, in the educational opportunities that exist, most of the focus is on how to avoid getting sued or how to not cause conflict in a real estate transaction.

Meanwhile, there's an enormous turnover rate for real estate professionals in the United States. Many reports show that over 75 percent of agents fail in the first year of business, and over 87 percent are out within three years. They simply aren't given the knowledge they need to survive.

What you really need—from the brand new Realtor® to the long-time professional—is education on lead generation, lead conversion, business development, sales mastery, marketing, financials, and what it's like to be a business owner. You're doing much more than selling real estate. You're a *business owner*—and we believe you have the potential to not only survive but also thrive in this profession.

WE'RE ALL IN THIS TOGETHER

We've found that there are two different types of personalities in real estate. There's the practitioner, who prioritizes the skills and training that will help them provide excellent service within their niche. And there's the entrepreneur, who recognizes that they own a business and need to expand their education and develop their business practices.

In this book, our goal is for the practitioner to expand their business and the entrepreneur to expand their practice. The difference comes down to mindset. And by the way, when we say "we," we're not just wagging our fingers at the collective "you." We include ourselves every step of the way, because we've been there. We have been in this business for more than twenty years each—Garry as an agent and Chris in marketing—and we're still practicing today.

WHO ARE WE?

Garry Creath, cofounder of The Paperless Agent, grew up around this kind of business—his parents were in real estate for forty-plus years together. But he fell into real estate entirely unintentionally back in 1997. Like many of us, his story begins with struggle.

After I graduated from Texas A&M, I left Texas and moved to Colorado to become a ski patroller. That was the plan. But one morning at 5:00 a.m., I got a phone call that changed everything.

My dad had unexpectedly died in the middle of the night.

My mom would have died of a broken heart without someone there to help her, so I left right away—no job, no plans. And I never moved back to Colorado. I stayed in Austin, and I did what any lost and wandering soul does: I got my real estate license.

More than twenty years later, Garry is still here—in both Austin and real estate. While working in real estate full time, Garry was taking six listing appointments per week, carried over fifty-six listings at a time, and was the co-owner of GoodLife Team, which won the Inman Innovator of the Year award. His real estate service and sales experience carries an emphasis on sales scripts, narratives, and processes for turning prospects into returning customers.

Chris Scott, president of The Paperless Agent, is a digital marketing expert who spent years helping real estate professionals market their databases to develop their real estate practices and ran the sales and marketing divisions for a two-time *Inc.* 500 award-winning company, all before running into Garry.

The rest, as they say, is history—and our histories share a common thread. Like Garry, though for different reasons, Chris also stumbled into real estate. From Chris:

I started off as an IT person and a computer programmer. Real estate was never in my plan. But it just so happened that I had worked in a company that was providing support and services to the real estate community. From there, I quickly moved into helping real estate professionals with marketing—beginning with Brian Buffini, who I worked with for eleven years.

Decades later, I'm still in real estate, working alongside Garry at Creath Partners and The Paperless Agent. But at the core of what I do—what drives me—is my passion for learning and sharing what I know. If I were to win the lottery, I'd become a full-time student. Learning has always been my passion.

It's Garry's decades of real estate experience and Chris's marketing savvy and love of learning and sharing information that makes our practice work and has led to the book you hold in your hands.

Garry has worked to overcome the struggles of falling into a real estate career, going all in—blood, sweat, and tears. (Almost undoubtedly the latter two, anyway, thanks to long hours in the office, well past the time the office managers would shut off the AC.) He knows the struggle and pressure that come with wondering whether the next deal will come before bills are due. He's been in survival mode, but he didn't want to stay there long. He learned all he could learn from the best he could find—literally listening at the door of Dee Shultz, his mentor, to hear how she worked—and did exactly what they did to get where they were.

Chris has plenty of success of his own to share—generating over 6,000 leads per month, managing pages with over 248,000 followers, and training over 50,000 Realtors® on social media marketing over the past three years. Chris holds the same two decades of experience in real estate, but from the valuable outside-in perspective of a marketer. Together, we're always in conversation about the books we're reading, the conferences we want to go to, and the ways we can continually improve our business for our customers.

Simply put, we all raise the industry together. There's no destination that ends your journey. We're all in this together, in a constant evolution of knowledge and practices combined with a good work ethic.

(DON'T) DO THE HUSTLE

There's a process that people have to go through to get from where they are to where they want to be. Maybe your life isn't what you want it to be. Maybe you're not performing in your work the way you'd want to perform.

For many of us, these thoughts tend to resurface every year around the beginning of January. You've taken time off to rest from a hard year, and you come back thinking, "I've got to get back to work." So you set objectives: "This year, I'm going to double my business—no, I'm going for ten times my business! I'm going all in, and I'm going to blow it out of the water!"

No doubt, you will hustle and work hard, as you've done every year. But when it comes down to it, how often have our strategies stretched beyond "I'm going to get down to work"?

Hustle has its place, but a real estate business is about more than that. First, there aren't enough hours in the day to be able to achieve an unreasonable goal. As we'll look at later in the book, your goals have to be substantiated by real, feasible action steps. Plus, the things you're doing and the systems required to sell twenty homes in a year are very different from those needed to sell a hundred in a year.

When you substantiate your goal, you might find that selling thirty-five homes is more feasible than a hundred, based on the number of calls you need to make, appointments you need to go on, contracts you need to convert, and closed deals you need in order to reach your goal.

But the other piece to that is if all you've got is hustle, you can easily hustle yourself right out of the business.

You could be doing the wrong activities altogether. As the proverb goes, "Optimism without knowledge is useless." It doesn't matter how optimistic you are—how much hustle you have; it's pointless if you aren't making the best choices.

There's no way to reach a 500 percent increase through a nondescript effort like "hustling" or "getting after it." Unlike most speakers and educators in this field, we won't expect you to turn motivation into miracles, and you shouldn't expect that of yourself, either. It doesn't work that way.

You're not going to hope your way into success, in real estate or in life.

WE WANT TO SEE YOU WIN

Tell us if this scenario is familiar: You're working your tail off. It's crazy how many hours you're working. You're sneaking work into every corner of your life— office hours all day long, and then clients want to see you in the evenings and on the weekends, always busy doing something. You know you're supposed to work hard, and you certainly feel like you are. You're worn out just from taking good care of your clients, so you figure the marketing tasks can slip a little if a day goes too long.

Come January, when you realize business needs to pick up to get you back on track, you hustle again to build it all back up. After you get a client or two, you pour yourself into taking really good care of them—just like you did for the clients you had last year. Prospecting activities slip again, and by the next year, you've hit the reset button yet again. Sure, you're getting to those clients who carry you through to a commission check—the national average is one per month—but then you've got nobody left. You're starting from zero, over and over again, and why? Because just blindly doing stuff won't get you results. It'll only get you burned out.

Everything we do has just one simple goal: to see you become a true business owner with a profitable, bountiful real estate business. Outside of our real estate business, we also run a real estate coaching, education, and technology company. We've trained over 71,000 real estate agents a year through our webcasts, giving them the tools they need to turn generic hustle into effective strategy. To stop hitting the reset button. To move from surviving to thriving in their real estate businesses.

To do that in this book, we'll go deeper than any of the conferences or education experiences you've had. We'll get into the tactical skills and thinking that someone who wants a long, successful career in real estate will need— and *only* what you actually need. Because there aren't enough hours in the day to grow your business to sell a hundred homes per year with the approach you've taken to hit a dozen homes per year. You're going to need to be intentional about the steps you take. We know, because we've been down that path already, and we want you to follow us there. We don't hustle anymore, because what does it even mean? No. You'll need a good work ethic, but more importantly you'll need to know the right things to do, and then you'll need to do those things. That's it.

Work through the book a chapter at a time, and we'll help you build your real estate business from the ground up—and we all know that you don't have to be just starting out to be back at ground level. If you already have an operating business, we'll help you refine your operation into an effective empire, à la Peter Drucker's *Effective Executive*: if you're doing the wrong thing efficiently, it's an exercise in futility.

Before we ever look at sales or realization, you'll design your platform and build intention into the services you offer your clients. We'll show you how to research your potential market and calculate its value as you set expectations and goals. Then we'll walk you through the sales and marketing skills that you need to succeed and—yes, we'll do some math—how to properly structure and track your finances.

Most importantly, you're going to walk away from this

book with a substantiated business plan. There are no pie-in-the-sky numbers here. By the end of the book, you'll know exactly who you're selling to, what you're selling, how much you can possibly sell, and what you need to do to get there.

Along the way, you'll have access to our website, www. BlueprintBook.Online, where you can print worksheets and supplemental information to put it all in action. If you'd still like hands-on help from there, our course is available to you as well. We've been where you are, and we've accomplished the goals that a lot of you are dreaming to. We're here to see you succeed. Are you ready? Let's go!

1

LAYING OUT THE BLUEPRINT

Garry's dad used to say, "I don't know where we're going, but we're making great time." Let's think about that for a second. Now, if you're starting off in LA and hoping to get to Washington, D.C., what happens if you don't know where that is? Perhaps if you head west, you'll find out pretty quickly that you've gone in the wrong direction. (That, or you'll take a boat and a really painfully long time to get there.) But if you don't have a plan and a destination, you'll likely be "making great time" in the absolute wrong direction.

It takes some intentionality to get where you want to go. You'll notice that as a recurring theme throughout this book: always checking in with yourself, your practice, and your clients to make sure you're where you need to be. But that level of intention starts much earlier than you might have realized. Namely, have you ever thought about what you provide your clients?

As real estate professionals, what is the actual service or product we render? Yes, homes and real estate are connected to what we provide clients, but it's not what we actually offer. In reality, when we're interacting with clients, from prospecting to closing a deal and beyond, we're not selling a property. We're selling a service.

If we were just selling homes, buyers wouldn't need us. Sellers wouldn't need us. It's not that complicated to identify a product that you want or a buyer who wants what you have. The service we render as real estate professionals is *associated* with products. It consists of recommending homes or properties to buyers, providing information and access to what's on the market, consulting with sellers on a home's value, marketing homes to buyers, and more.

But it's the services that we render that are the operational components to a real estate business. If we don't provide those services in a thoughtful way, then it becomes little more than labor. It's just opening the door or providing the paperwork. When we step outside of ourselves and our process to start providing thoughtful services to our clients, the business begins to transform.

You might have noticed by now that we tend to think a little bit differently about the scope of a Realtor® than what you might be used to. Whether you recognize it or not, when you set out to establish a real estate practice, you became an entrepreneur. We're businesspeople. And a business consists of three primary functions that we'll discuss throughout the book: sales and marketing, operations, and finance.

To run a successful real estate practice, every real estate professional should think of themselves as entrepreneurs who are managing a multifaceted business that needs attention on each of these functions. When you're an entrepreneur, you can't just focus on the operations of advising and consulting with clients to buy and sell homes. The operations, or services we render, become offers of help. Everything becomes an offer of value, and every offer of value should be designed with intention. An offer of help that has been designed with intention is a "point of value."

Designed points of value represent a change in principle from almost any other real estate process out there. You can go to seminars and listen to speakers who'll tell you to hustle, and you can learn all of the tactical tools that will help you generate leads or close deals. And we'll get into all of that throughout the book. But underneath all of those strategies in all of those chapters, we'll have this underlying principle of *designed value*.

Though every real estate professional shares some very basic mechanics of listing and selling in common, each real estate practice is its own unique business with its own unique business owner. As entrepreneurs, we want to look closely at the unique value that each of us can and does offer clients and then begin to design that value into our branding. A real estate business with designed value stands apart from its competition. It offers something new to customers and creates a superior experience that's worthy of the reviews, referrals, and repeat business that sustain a practice.

WHAT IS AN OFFER?

We all make offers to our clients. And by "offers," we don't mean an offer made to purchase a home. Nor do we mean "but wait, there's more!" or a direct offer to purchase some item or service. We're not talking about blinking lights and flashing signs. It can be, and usually is, much more subtle than that. Think of an "offer" as a way that you can provide help or service to your clients (past, prospective, and current). Dr. Fernando Flores gives us a definition of offer that we like to work from: *future actions to be performed that bring forth something missing, or new possibilities.*

That's really the key: offers open up the space of possibility. For that to happen, three factors have to be in place. First, we have to be sincere when we make the offer. Second, they have to *believe* that we are being sincere in our offer of help. And third, the offer of help must be relevant to what they care about.

Break it down this way. How much sincerity do you hear in a used car salesman's offer? Nothing against used car salesmen, but for the most part, the answer is "none." Even if someone comes along who's completely sincere in their offer of a new or pre-owned vehicle, it'll be difficult for the buyer—especially the prospective buyer—to believe it. They're just trying to sell another car to you, right?

All too often, however, we're just trying to sell another house. We're throwing out offers because it will help us, without investigating the wants, needs, concerns, and desires of our customers. The only way to build trust is to listen carefully and then—with sincerity and confidence—design valuable offers of help.

AUGUST IN TEXAS

The concept of offers has become the cornerstone of Garry's approach with clients. He's constantly listening and asking questions that might lead him to a new point of value to offer the client, and that has secured his place in the high-end luxury market in Austin.

Not long ago, Garry hosted an open house for a $2.75 million property, and he enlisted the help of some other agents for the event. Mostly, he tried to stand back and let the others engage, observing their interactions. One conversation in particular caught his attention. An agent walked up to a couple, said a few things to them, and then walked away.

Before following up, Garry caught the agent and asked what she offered them.

"Oh, I offered them water."

Now, it was August in Texas at the time, so water was a valid offer. (Water is often a valid offer.) That was a good move.

Then she said, "And I told them if they need anything they can just ask me."

Not-so-good move.

That's still an offer, but it's much weaker. As an open-ended offer, it's easy for people to decline it. And not only a direct decline—they can easily slip away unnoticed, without any confrontation.

"If you need anything..."

"Let me know if you have a question..."

"Just give me a call..."

These are common offers without any sort of design or intention built into them. A specific, valuable offer will make it easy to say yes. Of course they wanted water—it gets hot in Texas! That was a specific solution to a need they had, and it was easy for them to say yes and accept the offer.

When we offer to answer an unasked question, it leaves it to the client to figure out what they need to ask. They're always going to decline this offer, and it won't even be hard. When we design our offers with intention and value, we listen to them and their concerns, decide what might be of value to them, and connect all of those dots to make it easy for them. They don't have to figure any of it out on their own.

OFFERS SHOULD MEET A SPECIFIC NEED

When Garry realized what had happened between the agent and the couple, he obviously had to go meet them and investigate further. As always, his wheels were turning. *What can I offer? What questions can I ask to find out what will be valuable to them?*

He shook their hands, introduced himself as the host, and

then said, "I'm always curious how people hear about my open houses, because I market them in different ways."

The couple said that they lived just down the street and had gotten the postcard mailer he'd sent out.

Next question: "Ah, that's excellent! So are you thinking about moving?"

They weren't, but their friend was planning to relocate from Houston. They thought the house might work for him, so they were coming to check it out.

Garry spotted a point of value right away and offered it: "Why don't you give me the best email address where I can reach you. I have all of this great drone video and photography of the house and neighborhood. I can just send you all of it to pass along, so you don't have to take and send photos today. What's your best email address?"

The offer here is easy to say yes to. There's no gimmick or long-term commitment to ponder. There's great value— they could put their phones away and enjoy the open house and then still look awesome to their friend when they sent everything over. And it was sincere. Garry asked questions and listened to the answers to learn more about the couple, heard what it was they needed, and met that need with an offer of value.

DESIGNING OFFERS WITH INTENTION

Do you ever stop to think about how many promises you make to clients and prospects during the period of time you work with them? Sometimes those promises are overt—*I'm going to negotiate well on your behalf.* Others might be implied, like the way an advanced marketing strategy instills confidence that you'll market their home well.

Promises can be tangible—*if you sell your home with me and buy another in ninety days, I'll cover $5,000 of your closing costs.* Or your promises might go completely unsaid. You might demonstrate a promise to listen to them in the way that you relate to their situation and then confidently say, "I can help with that."

The idea behind this chapter, and ultimately the foundation of a solid real estate business, is that these promises shouldn't be accidental—they should be designed into your business. The promises that you make to your customers and that you imply to the marketplace of potential customers should be intentional, integrated into your brand, and specific to your market.

We aren't looking for "me too" type promises. Anyone can promise to work really hard for their customers. That's not designed value. The more tangible the value, the more relevant the offer will be for the people that you're working with.

Designed points of value are foundational to the rest of the work that you'll be doing. Before we can get into the granular tasks of marketing, sales, and business management that will come later in the book, we have to begin here, with an intentional design and clear points of value.

IDENTIFYING POINTS OF VALUE

The sum total of the promises you make your customers, or the points of value you offer them, is your brand or identity. Many of you are likely wondering whether you even have a brand or identity and where you should begin. That's okay. This isn't something people traditionally talk about in this industry. That's why we're working through these things together.

When your focus is on your real estate practice and not entrepreneurship, more often than not you end up starving for any kind of real estate sale you can get. You'll help anybody, anywhere. Unfortunately, that's not an asset to your business. It's a detriment. You can't differentiate yourself enough to sustain a business if you haven't defined what you want to offer. This is *exactly* why we need to design new points of value into how we connect, interact, and serve our customers.

> Designed points of value—offers of help—should be intentional, integrated into your brand, and specific to your market.

Creating new points of value requires that we first design the value. And designing the value requires making decisions on what we are going to design in the first place.

Regardless of the business that we're in, the goal is to take care of someone else's well-being in a really specific way. As Realtors®, we're taking care of our clients' shelters, futures, and families. The way you meet each of those needs will play out differently based on your own natural skills, the market you're working with, and where each client is in the life cycle of their interactions with you.

DESIGNING FROM YOUR STRENGTHS

There are a lot of ways to develop points of value, and a good place to start is where you feel most comfortable. This is often where your practice has drifted anyway, and working within your strengths allows you to be more authentic.

For example, some personalities are a bit more opportunistic and see opportunities everywhere, without really trying. Garry's got a point of value that can be considered *subconscious* or *embodied competence*. He's made so many specific tactics, strategies, scripts, and dialogues that they've become unconscious skills that just come out in conversation. He's always listening for cues and asking questions that might lead to an opening to use one of those tools. (You can see some of those skills play out in the questions and conversation prompts he shares in chapter 2.)

Sometimes designing an offer of help or a point of value just means changing the wording of something you're already doing. Someone with knowledge of the buying and selling process can package that information—which, hundreds of sales later, they likely know like the back of their hand—into a guide to offer to your clients. Or you might identify a feature of your process that you can present as an offer, such as an "easy exit, no questions asked" listing agreement. When you've identified the value you offer to home buyers and sellers, you can integrate it into your brand.

DESIGNING TO YOUR MARKET

Designed points of value can be so simple that you miss them—like offering water in August in Texas—or they can take an even higher form. For example, real estate investment consultation, property management, and leasing can all serve as new services and designed value. You might serve specific niche markets and price points, like urban core, luxury homes, senior living, first-time home buyers, and so on. There are Realtors® serving hundreds of clients each year, and all those clients are first-time home buyers. Whatever it is that you offer, design and build value into it.

If you've found yourself taking every opportunity that comes your way, designing points of value might be as global as switching your market to a specific type of client. Recently, we decided to specifically serve the luxury property market in Austin between $1 million and $2 million. That was a newly designed point of value that came from who we decided to market to.

If you don't yet know what that market might be or what you can offer it, think about the questions you find yourself answering regularly. If people are asking you for something over and over, it's a good indication that you've got a point of value to offer.

People would ask Garry, "How's the market?" Naturally, he'd respond with data and statistics and then find himself telling people about the investment properties he was buying. That would open a whole conversation about money available, the process, and whether they could do it, too. It took a while before he realized that was something he could offer.

DESIGNING FOR THE CLIENT

Points of value and offers of help start at the very top of your branding and move all the way through to the most granular levels, including what a client needs at a particular point in the relationship's life cycle. (And, to take just a second on that concept: yes, you do have branding. Think of it as simply who you are and who you market to.)

We've found that one of the most effective habits to adopt is to always seek to understand how you can make an offer of help. The only way to do that is to constantly ask questions to understand their situation. The offers that they need won't always be directly connected to sales, either, so you have to learn to listen for more than just home buying or selling cues.

Want to find out what someone is concerned about? Start with Facebook. There, you can see major life events—birth, death, marriage, new job—and design an offer around it. For example, someone posted on a Friday that they had soccer games on a Saturday. They said, "Man, it's gonna be brutally hot tomorrow. Wish I had a tarp." Garry happened to have a tarp and brought it over. That's a point of value in the relationship, and it stuck.

The other way to design points of value for a client life cycle is to map it out through the whole experience a client will have with you. This is a major focus of chapter 2, because it shows you unintentional points of value as well as pain points that can be addressed. Garry prefers to ask questions, and Chris likes to map out processes. That's probably why we work well together, because you can't have one without the other—especially if you want to innovate. We have to get analytical, ask questions about expectations and experience, and then evaluate the answers so that we can constantly improve the client's experience.

DESIGN REFLECTS CARE

The power behind true customer service is to sincerely and authentically care for your clients. Everything we're going to talk about throughout this book and everything we teach and speak about comes down to loving your people. Your job is to care about their concerns and hold them as yours. Take care of your clients, and make sure they know it. The only way they will know it is if you demonstrate it in your interactions, conversations, and offers.

When you know where your client is in their process and what they need, your offers will be more specific. The more specific your offer, the more it will be superior, which will create a bigger competitive advantage. Powerful offers that address what your clients want, need, and desire will lead to more accepted offers, and that will allow you to make even better offers. We're creating a continuous performance improvement loop that ultimately serves your market better than you or others have before.

It's not easy to design points of value, but in the next

chapter, we're going to analyze the offers you're already making, as well as two methods you can use to design better offers with more intention.

2

DESIGNING THE CLIENT EXPERIENCE

Readers, students, and colleagues often come to us looking for systems and processes that they can use to improve their businesses. They seek out seminars and classes that will give them that one tool or trick that will give them an edge. In reality, it often comes down to taking a step back and managing the client experience that you offer.

Points of value can be created, innovated, and offered across a huge range of interactions and services. Although it's important to design those points of value, most of us simply don't. A lot of times, we fall into services, offers, and habits without necessarily assessing the value of those things. But as real estate professionals, we are the managers of our businesses. If you truly want to be successful in this industry and you want to follow a process to get there, you have to develop some management skills and be proactive with the business you're developing.

We want you to develop these skills on your own so that you're not so reliant on others to give you a process or system, so we're going to work through two methods that can help you identify existing points of value and design new offers for your clients.

Garry's preferred method is to ask questions and gather information in every interaction with his clients—past, current, and prospective—to identify and meet their specific needs. The other method, which Chris prefers, is to map out your processes and the clients' experiences to identify and address pain points. Both are necessary, and they work hand in hand to help you step into your clients' shoes and determine which points of value you need to consider.

As entrepreneurs, this is a skill and an activity that we will want to invoke frequently. When you've acquired this skill, you'll be able to continuously evaluate and test new points of value in your marketplace.

METHOD #1: ASKING FOR HELP

The first method involves getting ideas, feedback, and help from our clients. Whether you've already designed points of value or not, it's important to know whether the customer experience lines up with your intentions. Sometimes, we miss points of value that are implied, or we think something is a good offer when it isn't. The only way to really find out is through active conversation. Conversations, customer surveys, and great listening skills can clue us in to what they need and where we can do better.

In other words, asking people what they want is a much more powerful way to determine their desires than guessing or assuming. In chapter 1, we talked a little bit about asking questions and listening to our people as we begin to design offers for them. It's easy to imagine asking these questions and listening to prospective buyers, but it's also important to go back to current and even past clients to gauge their experiences with you.

Using those asking and listening skills that we're constantly honing, we can talk to our current clients, past clients, or people in the market to buy and sell homes to learn more about where they are and how we can help. We don't necessarily want to ask them what they want, because they might not always know (remember to avoid "If I can help, let me know..."). Rather, we want to understand the problems they face so we can identify where to provide solutions.

Using structured questions, we can reveal gaps between their desired state and actual state, or gaps between perceived value and delivered value. Those gaps become the points of value we can create for our clients.

For example, surveys, interviews, or observation may reveal that clients are skeptical of the activities real estate agents take to market their homes. In response, we might offer a property marketing plan to address their concerns. The property marketing plan constitutes a point of value for our clients that distinguishes us from others.

IMPORTANT QUESTIONS TO ASK

- How was your experience?
- If I were a stranger asking you about your experience, what would you say?
- What could I have done better?
- Were there any expectations you had that I fell short of?

Surveys can't be your only method for gathering information, either. Going out for coffee and asking questions in a conversational mode will get you the most qualitative answers, hands down. Sit down with as many clients as you can. Identify where they're at in the life cycle, expose potential pain points and breakdowns, identify the root cause, and then work to solve that problem with a point of value.

WHOM TO APPROACH WITH QUESTIONS

It's important to look at the overall client experience, not only to identify the process but also to identify where a client is in their life cycle of working with you. Each conversation could represent a point of innovation that can increase your interaction with clients throughout that life cycle. Reach out to current clients, past clients, clients who haven't worked with you in a long time, and prospective clients. All of their perspectives have value.

What you learn from one phase might inadvertently help you with the others. For example, if you're talking to prospective clients and find a common problem—maybe there is a recurring confusion about how you'll market and sell their home—you can design a point of value to address those concerns. Then that solution could spill over to help other clients as well.

At one point, we realized that there were a significant number of homeowners with expired listings. Clearly, there had been a breakdown somewhere that kept their properties from selling. So we looked for the common threads and then created an eight-week marketing plan designed for those clients specifically—anyone who had expired listings. The marketing plan solved that breakdown not only for them but also for every potential home seller that we would work with. It was a designed offer of help that addressed a part of the client experience that comes before they work with you.

When you talk with someone who has already worked with you, the things that they care about will be vastly different from those a prospective client cares about. Do you need to add value that can increase the frequency of working with them? Do you need to increase your chances of working with new clients? Do you need to do something that will increase your chances of referrals? In looking for these answers, not only will you learn more about what your clients experience and need, but you'll also influence a better dynamic between you and your past clients.

In fact, if you ask these questions before someone gives a testimonial, you're probably going to enhance the testimonial that they would have given you. You're showing that person that you actually care about them. The number one thing that people want from you is to feel like they are being heard. If you can show them that you aren't just hearing them but actively listening to them, they'll be much more satisfied with the interaction.

LISTEN BEFORE YOU SPEAK

When you're face-to-face with a client and ready to ask some questions, remember that asking the *right* question matters just as much as reaching out in the first place. You can't get a clear picture of their experience or be relevant with offers without first listening and asking the right questions.

A quick way to gauge your actual offer of listening is to think about how much you're talking in a given interaction. When you're making offers to someone, if you speak more than 10 percent of the time, you're doing it wrong. Ask a question, and then let them speak. If you're talking too much, back up with a "Can you tell me more about that?" or "That seems really important to you. Would you share more about that with me?"

Without listening to their experience and perspective first, you're going to ask the wrong questions. Think about the couple from the open house in chapter 1. "Do you like the house?" would mean very little to them, because they weren't looking to buy. The wrong question will then lead to the wrong offer. An irrelevant question leads to irrelevant offers.

> Listen to understand, not to respond.

QUESTIONS TO HELP YOU DIG DEEPER

The right questions asked in the right way can help you understand the client's actual experience and can give you ideas on how to better design points of value. You can use these questions on your own to get introspective and realistic about what you're actually offering or directly ask past clients, active clients, or prospects about their experiences.

This might be a scary prospect for you, especially asking questions of your past customers. It's okay. You've produced a better experience for them than you might think. Read that again, because it's important to hear: you've produced a better experience than you think. Believing that will build your confidence. Still, even if you can't reach out to clients yet and you start by only asking yourself the questions, you'll be much farther along than you would be without asking them at all.

The right questions force you to look more closely at the points of value and pain points that exist in your process so that you can begin to design them with more intention and implement them more effectively. Here are some that you can start with:

- With all the agents and firms out there, why did you choose to work with us?
- When you decided to work with me and my firm, what

were your expectations going into the process? (Or, what are my clients often asking for and looking for when they come to me?)

- Now that you've purchased or sold your home, can you provide specific examples of how those expectations were or were not met? (Or, where are my clients often struggling or hesitant?)
- What did you find frustrating about the buying or selling experience? What made it so frustrating? (Or, are there points where I seem to "lose" clients—where I'm doing extra work or running into roadblocks with them?)
- What did you wish we would have done to make our service over the top? (Or, if I do actually lose clients, who are they turning to instead, and what are they seeking out?)
- For a prospect who chose to work with someone else, why did they choose to work with them?

The important thing is to not settle for deflective answers. If they say that they decided to work with a family member, find out why they felt that family member was more competent than you to perform the service. What did they stand to gain by working with that person over you? The more clearly they can specify their reasons, the more you will learn.

HOW TO ASK GOOD QUESTIONS

Because you don't want to settle for incomplete answers, this method really can't be accomplished with a survey. You need to at least make a phone call, but going out for coffee and asking the person questions in a conversational mode will get you the most qualitative answers. Over an in-person meeting, you're looking them in the eye, you're communicating with body language, and they get to see your competence in action.

By contrast, a survey is cold. It's clear that you're just trying to collect data and nothing more—it's a favor that you're asking them to offer you. Plus, let's say your survey asks whether someone would be interested in more information. Even if they answer "yes," you don't know whether their yes is an "Uh, yeah?" or a solid "Yes, absolutely."

When you're sitting across the table or having coffee with someone, you can't help but pick up on all of that nonverbal communication. What's more, people want to spend time with you! If you can give that time as a gift and then provide secondary offers as well, the effect will be much more powerful than a cold survey and some follow-ups. As you guide the conversation with intentional questions, you'll get more qualitative information to fuel your innovation.

METHOD #2: MAPPING THE PROCESS

Because both of these methods are intertwined and both are necessary, one doesn't really come before the other. You can do them at the same time, or you can favor the one that you enjoy more. Either way, you'll need to work through both feedback and mapping to get the best picture of your practice in action.

Mapping out the existing client experience is an important step. Basically, you're going to look at something that you currently offer and then think critically about it. This helps us see what it is we're actually offering. Often, we don't need to innovate a new point of value at all—we just need to get more intentional with something that we might not have realized we offer.

Not long ago, we realized that we were regularly offering

education around real estate investment. So we set out to create a bigger-picture point of value, and we began to intentionally help clients buy and sell investment homes. In this case, we didn't have to ask Garry's prior customers whether they needed this service, because they were the ones asking for it.

If you find yourself repeating information or helping people with the same thing over and over, you've probably got a point of value that can be designed and used more effectively.

DRAWING A PROCESS MAP

Process mapping can intertwine with feedback by walking through your client's experience to identify areas for improvement. A way to accomplish this is to make a literal map or blueprint of the process associated with some part of your clients' and prospects' interactions with you. Then examine and criticize each point of interaction to see what can be improved.

For example, one part of your client experience happens before they contact you. It's highly likely, even if they are a past client, that your client will search for information about you on the internet. A process map lays out every single step of that process from their perspective.

Typical Real Estate Transaction from Listing to Close

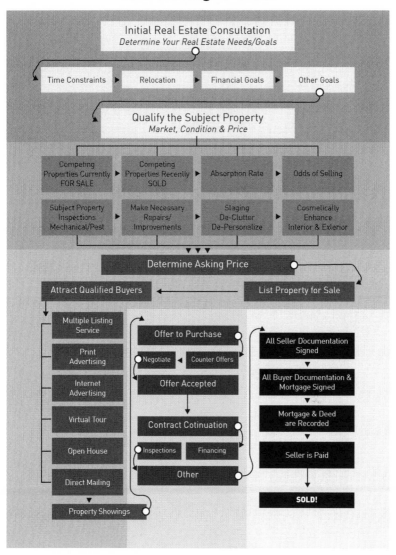

Initial Real Estate Consultation
Determine Your Real Estate Needs/Goals

Time Constraints ▶ Relocation ▶ Financial Goals ▶ Other Goals

Qualify the Subject Property
Market, Condition & Price

Competing Properties Currently FOR SALE ▶ Competing Properties Recently SOLD ▶ Absorption Rate ▶ Odds of Selling

Subject Property Inspections Mechanical/Pest ▶ Make Necessary Repairs/Improvements ▶ Staging De-Clutter De-Personalize ▶ Cosmetically Enhance Interior & Exterior

▼ ▼ ▼

Determine Asking Price

Attract Qualified Buyers ◀ List Property for Sale

- Multiple Listing Service
- Print Advertising
- Internet Advertising
- Virtual Tour
- Open House
- Direct Mailing

▼ Property Showings

Offer to Purchase
Negotiate ◀ Counter Offers
Offer Accepted
Contract Cotinuation
Inspections Financing
Other

All Seller Documentation Signed
▼
All Buyer Documentation & Mortgage Signed
▼
Mortgage & Deed are Recorded
▼
Seller is Paid
▼
SOLD!

The next step is to analyze the experience to determine whether it is a positive experience or one that could use improvement. In the previous example, if a client's search for you doesn't turn up results, a point of value you can create is to improve your online presence so that you're better represented online and your clients can contact or refer you with confidence.

THE CUSTOMER EXPERIENCE MAP

A key to identifying specific processes to address for innovation is to analyze your complete client experience and search for areas of improvement. Most experience maps in a real estate practice will look somewhat similar, with those shared touchpoints that we all seem to have.

CLIENT EXPERIENCE

STAYING IN TOUCH · REPEAT OR REFERRAL · VISITS WEBSITE · FINAL CLOSING · FIRST CONTACT · TRANSACTION MANAGEMENT · BUY/SELL EXPERIENCE · FIRST APPOINTMENT · INITIAL CONSULTATION

Look closely at each step of the experience and ask yourself or your clients thoughtful questions about them. What points of value can you offer at each of these steps?

In this loop of questions and analysis, everything that we're able to address with someone leads to the next thing we can address. When the agent at Garry's open house offered water, it opened the door for a conversation so that the agent could learn what to do to be of help to that couple.

As we also learned from that open house in August, asking, "What can I do to help?" or telling them to reach out with questions won't get you any answers. When listening and understanding come first, we're able to make offers of real and valuable help that open doors for more potential value, help, and client satisfaction.

With an idea of how to identify points of value and to think critically about your practice, let's look at some specific types of offers that you might want to incorporate.

GOOD QUESTIONS AND THE ONLINE INQUIRY

Let's think about one of the worst of the worst-case scenarios for any Realtor® and reverse engineer it: the online lead. When someone inquires about a specific property, we get a standard email. The most common response a

Realtor® will send back is, "Here's the property. Let me know if you have any questions about it; let me know if you want to go see it."

But, like the agent's question at Garry's open house in chapter 1, that's a weak offer. It allows the person to disappear silently. Most likely, the offer isn't even relevant at the moment. They're exploring possibilities, and the possibility of going to a showing isn't even on the table yet.

So what *do* they want? Well, they might want to gather a lot of information from a lot of different sources. They might want more photos. They might be looking for properties that aren't "on the market," so to speak. In most markets right now, homes that are a good deal are moving pretty quickly, so it's important to be able to know what's coming and catch it fast. Not all homes even show up on syndicated sites, which leads to consumers thinking people are misrepresenting information. They simply don't know whom to trust.

A more specific offer in that situation, then, might look like this:

> *If you're interested in this home, here's my number. Please text me, and I'll send you more photos or take you to a showing. However, if this home does not meet your needs, please know that I have a direct buyer program. That program gives you*

direct access to our MLS, and it gives you direct access to the homes I know are coming on the market that are not yet available for sale.

This message relays valuable information that the buyer is not going to get anywhere else, and it's probably just a repackaged offer that you've been providing all along.

How can they have direct access to the MLS? You simply set up a search for them. That's it. Then they'll have direct access to accurate, up-to-date listings, which they can't get on their own on syndicated sites. For homes that aren't yet on the market, there's often a "coming soon" status in the MLS, Facebook groups about houses soon to be on the market, and networking groups as well.

Another unique and powerful offer you can make buyers is to contact expired or withdrawn homes that meet a buyer's criteria. Those sellers were interested in selling their home at some point in the past, which means bringing them a qualified and motivated buyer could be the right offer of help to them, too!

None of that is possible without asking the right questions, knowing your process, and designing points of value to offer at just the right time.

AN IMPORTANT ASIDE: ONLINE REPUTATION

According to the National Association of Realtors®, over 95 percent of buyers start the search for their properties online. Both your presence online and your web savvy offline will make a difference. The more information you have when you talk with your sellers, the more confidence they'll have in you and your ability to drive traffic and find buyer interest. They'll trust you to deliver on your promises.

In evaluating our own client experiences, we've realized that when someone is about to choose whom they're going to work with—or if they are deciding whether to refer you—their decision will be based on what they can find out about you online. This phenomenon is specific to real estate and backed not only by our experience but also by research.

In real estate, when someone is thinking of referring you, they consider your online presence just as much as your offline presence before they decide to work with you *or* refer you. Why? They know that whomever they refer you to is going to look you up online as well, and one of the top reasons people choose their real estate agent is the agent's reputation. They don't want to refer someone who has a poor reputation or bad online presence, even if their own experience with you was great.

Even if someone has a word-of-mouth referral, they'll

verify that referral by doing a Google search first. When you look at the National Association of Realtors® profile of home buyers and sellers, the number one thing home sellers want us to do is to market their homes—but they'll base their decision on our online reputation, not just the marketing promises we make.

For this reason, analyzing your Google search results is an important point of research. If they're not great, that's a place to start designing a point of value. This matters for prospective clients, of course, but in light of what we know about referrals, it's also important for the life cycle remaining for past clients. They want to look good when they give a referral, which means you have to look good online.

MORE OFFERS YOU MIGHT DESIGN

The entire listing appointment is an offer, of course, but there are micro-offers all the way through that build on each other. One offer is to document everything that you're talking about, the photos in the house, the improvements that might get the highest rate of return, or the improvements that aren't worth the effort at all. Offer to help the seller understand what a buyer is willing to pay for their home. Help them understand where buyers are and what "someone" needs to do to market their home—which can lead to an offer of marketing services as well.

You might even be able to offer the idea that it's not the right time to move. Offers always should have value to clients, even when there's no immediate benefit for you.

A simple but profound point of value that can affect your online reputation and help your clients is to position yourself as a real estate expert. When we send out newsletters, they are real estate specific and, more specifically, real estate *stats* specific. Why? Because when you're talking to your clients and offer statistics, you're offering relevant information that places you in a position of expertise and authority in your field. People look at statistics as indisputable. They trust the stats; therefore, they trust you.

Other data that will instill confidence in your ability is the background information about a deal. Buyers want to know that they're getting a good deal when they make an offer. How do you know whether a home is a good deal? You can look up sold data in the area. In nondisclosure states, at least, you have to be a customer to get that information from a Realtor®, which means you can offer something that moves them forward in their life cycle as your client.

Past clients need offers, too. Once a year, the tax assessor tells everyone what their homes are worth and what they might be taxed at for the coming year. That's a huge opportunity to reach out to everyone you've worked with to say, "Hey, I just got my tax assessment. I don't know about you, but I'm going to protest mine. Let me help you protest yours."

While you're doing that full market analysis for anyone who accepts the offer, you can look them up in the MLS to see when they bought their house. Statistically speaking, people move every three to seven years. If someone has been there three years or more, come back to them with that analysis and say, "Great news. This is what a buyer is willing to pay for your home right now. Instead of fighting your taxes, maybe it's time to make a move."

DESIGN CLIENT-BASED OFFERS FIRST

A client of Garry's was under contract to make an $800,000 purchase when a property tax assessment came through with bad news. His tax bill was going to increase his mortgage by $400/month, and his cash at closing would jump to about $27,000. He loved the house, and everything else was in line, but he was going to be cash poor and wasn't comfortable with that idea.

Instead of having him forge on, Garry advised him to take a step back, get out of the deal, and go find something that would be more suitable. The difference there really doesn't show up until about a year later. Will the client be in that home you encouraged, pinching pennies, blaming you for pressing them into the deal? Or will they be in a house they love, grateful for your direction, and thinking of you as a trustworthy advisor?

When you take a step back to think about the bigger picture, this whole process is not just about the photos, listings, and little details. It's about helping clients make the right decision. Sometimes, that decision might be to wait. Your role is to give people the very best information they need to make a decision, and sometimes the boost they need to guide that decision.

Take the time to map out your processes to see how it all actually works. Ask questions of yourself and your clients to look more closely than you ever have before. Use that information to improve existing points of value, design new offers, and provide solutions for pain points.

Laying this foundation—and constantly revisiting it as long as you are in business—is the differentiator for thriving real estate practices. We've worked together on these methods for a long time. Trust us, trust the process, and let's work through it together, step-by-step.

SOMETHING TO THINK ABOUT

Think about a point of value that you would like to add to your business. Why would this be an effective point of value for you to offer? How would it provide superior service? Why would clients find this point of value useful, attractive, or helpful? Visit www.BlueprintBook.Online for more on working through points of value.

3

FINDING GOLD

On National Geographic, there's a show called *Yukon Gold,* which follows gold miners up in Canada. Shows like this that give us a glimpse into other industries are fascinating. When else would most of us get to know what a day in the life of your average Canadian gold miner looks like? Watching the series, a clear pattern emerges: they're mining gold, yes, but it's not really about the gold. No. Those guys are all about profit.

Instead of finding the right plot of land and hoping that's where they will strike gold, they're constantly looking for dirt, water, and ways to keep their gold dredges and generators running. As long as that dredge is shaking down water and dirt, they're doing all right. They can stand to think about other things like location and results. But if it goes down even for five minutes, panic ensues. Every minute they aren't shaking, they're losing money. It's not about striking gold—it's about shaking the dirt and water down through the dredge.

In real estate, people are often looking for that shiny object. They keep moving around, trying to get those big, quick results. But there's a process to finding gold in real estate, and it's very methodical. Finding gold isn't about getting lucky; it's about the process.

USING CREDIBILITY AND TRUST TO HELP US DIG DEEP

In the process of identifying and maximizing opportunities for ourselves, the research we're going to do will provide a massive point of value for our clients. When we can offer insight to our clients—when we can communicate specific knowledge of their needs and solutions in a relevant way—it builds an enormous amount of trust. If Chris can tell a client that the median income for senior buyers is $66,700 and that the median age of senior buyers is sixty-seven, the client has to wonder: what else might he know?

On the flipside of that, having that information can change the way we design points of value in the first place. People purchasing senior housing aren't eight-five and ninety. They're sixty-seven. Sixty-seven is not old. How might that information change how we market or what our approach might be? Which tools and technology can help us to address that trend?

Let's back up a step further. Say you've been thinking of developing a home buyer guide to offer as a point of value in your business. After doing some research, you notice that many of the homes for sale in your market are move-up homes—those where the person buying it likely owned a home before. Perhaps they're exactly in the demographic of those boomers, or they're looking for more space or to live in a different part of town. When you identify that information, knowledge in hand, you can make a note of the trend that your database potentially reflects. Then you can modify your home buyer guide to be specific to your market: the "Move-Up Home Buyer's Guide," tailored to just the right demographic.

The message and some of the services for this buyer will be very different than for a first-time buyer or the downsizing or economizing buyer. This means the content of the guide would have to shift, and you'd promote the guide a bit differently in order to bring people in who would be interested in moving up.

Another example of applying research to a specific target market is to look at local areas. If you find that a certain area has enough turnover, big enough price-bands, and no clear market dominators, you might make that market a new area of focus. Your home buyer guide, again, can be tailored to that market.

Thinking back to *Yukon Gold,* we can see our own processes beginning to emerge. We can isolate some key components—to shake out the details, if you will—to find that three Ts emerge: tools, tech, and trends. Just like the gold miners are constantly honing their processes, we can focus on these components to move us closer to our goals.

TOOLS

Sixty years ago, a carpenter would use a hammer and nails to build a house. In fact, *every* carpenter would use a hammer and nails to build a house. You were only as productive as your own skill and speed could make you. But one day, in 1950, a single tool hit the market and changed everything. Anyone who used the pneumatic nail gun could suddenly shoot as much as a nail a second with much less effort than they'd ever expended. Their productivity could increase from nothing more than using a more effective tool.

More recently, dentists saw their own shift. After long years of referring their patients to orthodontists for rubber bands and expanders and cement and brackets, the Invisalign tool offered a new opportunity. Now dentists can sell alignment services directly to many of their patients, who can then go through a much simpler process to get their teeth straightened. The process becomes better for the dentist and the patient—as long as the dentist learns how to understand and use this new tool.

The tools available to us in real estate aren't as clear and tangible as nail guns or Invisalign, and there are many to choose from. If we pay attention, some of them—but not all of them—can create similar opportunities to increase business. For example, your listing presentation itself is a potential tool for turning more appointments into contracts. If you have an effective listing presentation or format, you can tweak and use it to build trust and lock in more clients. It'll improve your ability to go on listing appointments and to then turn more of those appointments into signed agreements for you to list their homes.

Sometimes, tools come in a more obvious shape: technology. One tech-based tool that everybody should have is a database. In the old days, database "technology" would have looked like a desktop Rolodex. These days, that's no longer sufficient. Now we use a CRM (contact relationship management) system. It allows us to turn more of the people in our database into ongoing relationships that produce referrals and repeat business. CRM is technology, but, more importantly, it's a tool for our businesses.

One of our practices in identifying opportunities is constantly scanning the horizon for tools we should incorporate, tools we should upgrade, and tools we should learn how to use better. It's not necessarily productive or advisable to just keep jumping to the next new tool.

For example, you might have a tool for listing presentations, but how good are you at communicating those scripts? How effective are you when you use that tool? It takes time to adapt and to really hone your use of tools, and that is time well spent.

TECHNOLOGY

A lot of times, technology drives the development of tools. And there are certainly tools to be used that are rooted in technology. But technology in and of itself offers a lot for us to be able to find gold within our businesses. For example, there are some powerful advertising tools and technologies out there, like the ability to run ads on Facebook, Instagram, Google, or YouTube. But within those platforms, each of them is a way to communicate with more people. They allow us to expand our influence while spending less time and less money than ever before.

As with tools, we have to constantly scan the horizon for new technologies to embrace and ways to improve our use of the technology we have. (Imagine being the last builder to get a nail gun!) We're always teaching folks about technologies because we know that they are just out of reach for most people. If you can spend just a little bit of time learning the right tech and tools, you're going to find more gold in your business. It's like the gold miners who are constantly working on their machines. If new technology allows for twice the amount of dirt to churn out twice the amount of gold, that's what they're going to upgrade to. But they have to pay attention, as we do, to the improvements available.

TRENDS

You might take an entire day to read this book. At the same time, on YouTube, users will watch over a billion hours of video. That's right—*billion with a B*. That's not just a fad. More hours are spent on YouTube on a daily basis than on Netflix and Facebook combined. That's the kind of trend that we need to learn how to use before it becomes a missed opportunity.

Instead of conducting your own market research to track trends, like so many industries must do, you have access to thorough, detailed, relevant statistics published every month. Without digging into the data provided by organizations like the NAR (National Association of Realtors®) and your local Board of Realtors®, many of us never realize the opportunities ahead that are often right at our fingertips.

For example, if you log into nar.realtor and then navigate to Research and Statistics, you'll have a number of free reports or reports that have just a small fee attached to them. All of the reports are divided by categories. There are housing opportunities and market experience surveys, and full buyer and seller profiles that can be broken down by demographics—by buyers with kids or by subregion, for example. We can dial it down to not only our state but also our metropolitan statistical area to get a full economic and real estate market report.

If you're feeling a little intimidated by the idea of research, it might help to reframe this exercise a bit. When you sit down to find new information or learn a little about your market, take a deep breath, and try to approach it from a curiosity standpoint rather than research. As you read, filter everything through the lens of "How can I benefit from this information?"

Sometimes just a headline or sentence is enough to benefit your practice. Other times, you'll become engrossed in the data or analysis and want to take it all in. The great thing about this kind of research is that no one is over our shoulders, grading us on our efforts. This is simply another way of being curious, looking at the market from a different angle, and identifying the best ways to benefit our customers and our businesses.

EMBRACING CORRECTION

As you build your gold-finding machine out of relevant

tools, tech, and trends, you'll start to shake down your market and methods to discover new areas of focus. When we were doing some MLS research not long ago, we uncovered a market for $1 million–$2 million homes. When we realized that 95 percent of the luxury and high-end homes that sold in Austin fell into that price range, we began modifying our message to appeal specifically to those in that range. That move made sense and has worked out well for us.

But that's not always how the story goes. One of the most overlooked ways of being able to identify a micro-trend within a business is to embrace correction. Usually, that comes in the form of negative feedback. Someone says something, or, more dramatically, the market outright rejects something you're doing. Something isn't going the way you wanted it to, and it's not going well on a repeated basis. That's a correction.

A lot of times, we won't even acknowledge the correction. We don't do anything with it at all. In fact, Garry learned this with a neighborhood called Lost Creek, local to us, which was a market he'd wanted so badly to break into. For five years, he kept working at it, investing time and money and effort trying to make something happen. Looking back, we ran the numbers and realized he'd invested over $78,000 trying to penetrate that market. Do you know what he got in return? Absolutely nothing. Zero ROI. He didn't sell one single house in that whole neighborhood.

For all of that planning, he'd missed a small but significant detail: two other Realtors® held over 70 percent market ownership.

It's all too easy to see that sort of thing as a challenge. It's something to conquer, right? Pride sneaks in and says, "I can beat this sucker. I don't care what it's going to take. I don't care what I have to sacrifice. I'm going to *hustle*, and I'm not going to lose."

Well, okay. But the problem was that Garry was getting consistent feedback over time. He was *absolutely* going to lose. There was no way to actually compete there. We couldn't have sold enough homes to make money that justified the effort. All of that time, energy, and money had been wasted in that farm, when we could have just done the research up front to see whether it was a viable opportunity. It had never been worth pursuing.

When you get those corrections—those clear messages that you've got no businesses doing that thing you're doing—embrace it! Take that energy and money somewhere else, and be grateful that you got the message before you sank tens of thousands of dollars into it.

Interestingly enough, when Garry gave up on Lost Creek and instead took the very same approach (and a much smaller budget) in a neighborhood called French Place, he wound up with a 40 percent market share within twelve months.

That's the key here. We can't take correction as a chastisement and just lick our wounds and move on. Embracing it is the key. We have to turn that correction into something. This isn't like running a Facebook campaign and then shrugging it off as "it doesn't work for me" (we've learned that lesson too). Real estate runs in a ninety to 120-day cycle. It takes that long to see results. A lot of people will give up before that cycle is complete. Just as many will quit that activity completely when they give up, without trying to figure out how to go about things differently to make it work for them.

Too many of us just stop the strategies we were using when our own Lost Creeks don't work out. It must have been the mailings or the events or whatever it is we were doing. But the same exact strategy that bombed in Lost Creek worked amazingly well in French Place, for a fraction of the cost.

Embracing the correction requires—again—curiosity: digging to identify the correction and how we can embrace those lessons and adjust moving forward.

PUTTING IT ALL INTO PRACTICE

Let's take a look at research in practice, using the tool of the NAR resource database to discover trends that we can address with tech in hand. So the first report to look at when you dig into the research available to you is the NAR's recent home buyers and sellers report. Every year, the NAR conducts a massive survey and publishes the data for us to use. This is vital information that can shape everything from the offers you design to the type of practice you build. Even if you aren't a data person, this is the singular resource that can be a game changer all on its own.

When you access this report, which is easy to find on the NAR website, you'll see a few highlights on the main page. Right away, you'll have a good amount of information to process. You'll see how many buyers were first-time home buyers, as well as the average ages of first-time and repeat buyers. You'll see demographic information, how often people are using agents, and any sort of notable shift from the previous year or from historical trends.

After you've downloaded the full report, however, things start to get juicy. There's no way to process all of this information at once, so you might tackle it in a couple of different ways. You can keep it on hand and look up data related to a specific service you already offer or one you have in mind. Do the trends reflect what you're trying to offer? Does it make sense to keep that as a point of value, or should it be adjusted a bit to match the ways that people are actually buying and selling?

Or you might read through a section at a time with a bit of curiosity. What catches your eye? What surprises you? What's something you didn't know? What's something that supports an offer of help that you've already designed?

The key is to look for something that can improve a point of value or spark some creativity for designing something new. For example, if the report shows a buyer profile termed "married with kids," it will have some demographics listed out within that category. Now let's say only 32 percent of married-with-kids couples are first-time buyers. If that's true, then the remaining 68 percent are *not* first-time home buyers.

If you're reading with curiosity and that catches your eye, you'll relate it to that buyer guide you've been thinking about making. Then you'll remember all those married-with-kids profiles you have in your database, or the families that you've served. Instead of a regular home buyer's guide, maybe you need a move-up buyer guide with a family focus, addressing more of the concerns that the folks who fit this profile might have, including school reports, a map of local parks, family-friendly restaurants, and so forth.

Millennials are now the vast majority of first-time home buyers, at 66 percent in 2015, with generation X behind them at 26 percent. Both of these generations are comfortable online, particularly millennials, because they grew up with the internet. Though previous generations would contact a real estate agent first, today's buyers are finding their homes online almost exclusively. Fully 99 percent of millennials search for homes online, and half of all buyers cited finding the home as the most difficult step of the process.

Already, we can see that it's not enough to have your contact information available online. Buyers need to have access to excellent listings with your contact information attached. If your firm doesn't have a website already, you're in the minority and at a complete disadvantage. Property listings on your firm's website should be accessible and high value. Excellent photos are no longer preferable but rather required, and slightly higher-tech options like interactive maps, neighborhood information, and video walk-throughs are becoming more and more important as well.

In addition to listings, buyers are using sites for agent profiles, mortgage calculators, information about the process, and community information. At each point of the home-buying process, you have an opportunity to design an offer of help for a vast majority of clients who want to use your website as a resource.

In spite of the overwhelming demand for technological points of value, nearly half of all firms cited "keeping up with technology" as one of their biggest challenges. In fact, of the one billion people on Instagram, only 14 percent of real estate professionals are utilizing it. There's a massive opportunity to exploit here. These research *tools* make the *trend* clear: practices that have a handle on *technology* as an offer of help can gain access to largely untapped opportunities.

GO WHERE THERE'S VALUE

We're always looking to the future to think about how things are changing and shifting. The way that we sell real estate today might be different in five years. It's changing all the time. For example, nearly everyone communicates with their clients via smartphone or email, but younger Realtors® are expanding their online offers to include blogs and vlogs. You might also notice that buyers are looking for video of the home about half of the time, but fewer than half of Realtors® are using drones to capture these images. If clients are there and other real estate professionals are not, that's exactly where your opportunities can be found.

But this doesn't mean you have to be everywhere. The

common denominator among tools, tech, and trends is simple: it's you. It comes down to what you need to do for your practice and your market and your effort. Other industries spend thousands to millions of dollars on market research to gather in-depth pictures of where their potential clients are and where opportunities lie. For real estate professionals, the data is already there. In the next chapter, we'll learn how to take all of this information and translate it into cost and value so that you can decide what to implement and what to put on the back burner. But as with any entrepreneur and their business, *you* are the ultimate deciding factor.

Will you take the time to invest in researching new tools and technology? Will you take the time to invest in learning how to use these things? Will you take the time to understand the trends in our industry or within your local marketplace? And then, what will you do with that information? What steps will you take to identify your opportunities and turn them into gold?

SOMETHING TO THINK ABOUT

Spend some time with the NAR reports for your area and with your existing tools and tech. Where do you see new or untapped opportunities? If you examine your practice, can you spot any "Lost Creek" situations that might be communicating a correction?

4

GOLDEN OPPORTUNITIES

There's an agent on the East Coast—Brenda—who had been in the business for several years when she came to us. Real estate, not surprisingly, was her second career. She was selling about $12 million annually at the time and wanted to get up to $30 million. So far, so good. That's a fairly common story: second career, getting your feet under you, and wanting to really start to settle in. In many cases, that tends to look like "I want to double my sales."

As with anyone in that situation, we asked her, "What are you planning to do between now and then?" She didn't know. All she knew was that she needed our help. Fair enough.

So, first things first, before we could determine where she

needed to go, we needed to see everything she was doing. Her current business plan; how she was marketing herself to her database and reaching out to the people who already knew, trusted, and liked her; how she was staying in touch and how often; how she was networking—all of it.

"That's easy," she said. "I'm not doing anything, really."

I'm sorry, what now?

"The business just seems to come to me, I guess. I know a lot of people at my daughter's school. We talk, they tell me they're looking to buy or sell, and it sort of just happens. I've never sent an email. I don't have a database. I'm just not doing anything."

Twelve million bucks sold a year, without doing a thing. *Okay, then.*

On the other hand, an agent here in Austin had been in business about as long as Garry, and she had catapulted into success as one of the top ten real estate professionals. In 2000, where Garry was selling $18 million, this woman was selling more like $50 million. For a while, that was inspiring.

Garry reached out to his mentor and said, "I want to get there. I want to do what she's doing." But she encouraged him to look a bit more closely.

"You're just looking at sales, Garry. That's the wrong metric." When you ignore the amount on the checks or listed as sales, the truth came out: she wasn't making any more money than Garry. She wasn't making a million dollars a year; she was *spending* a million dollars on advertising and marketing, taking loss after loss. It's fine if you want to do that and have the ability to, of course, but do it with your eyes wide open.

On the surface, Brenda was doing remarkably well, but it was on a shaky foundation, and she wasn't where she wanted to be. She could see a target in front of her and had no idea how to get there. In this chapter, we'll dive in with our eyes wide open. You'll learn how to value the opportunities you've identified in previous chapters— weighing that gold you've found—and how to pursue the ones that will get you where you want to go.

WE'RE NOT HERE TO GAMBLE

There's no wrong way to identify and maximize opportunity, really. What works for you might not work for us, and vice versa. It takes that curious mindset we talked about in chapter 3 in order to keep digging for opportunities. And then we've got to work to rationalize and substantiate each one that we uncover to determine whether they're worthwhile. Sometimes, that takes a little bit of trial and error—and a whole lot of embracing correction.

Valuing opportunities is a constant exercise for both of us, always looking for ways to evaluate opportunities, improve them, and calculate their costs. We've broken it down as far as knowing how many new customers we'd need each month in order to warrant the investment. In other words, though there's some risk involved in the trial and error, we know what a new customer means for our business, and that helps us weigh our costs and carefully plot out those "risks."

Not long ago, for example, we considered partnering with Google. We wanted to do a three-month project where Google would build campaigns for us. We first started with the cost per ad and then determined what return we'd need in order to make it worthwhile. The numbers seemed to make sense at first, but the more we looked at it and calculated the cost, the more we started to realize the scope of the additional opportunities that would have to occur in order to make it work. We realized it was a pretty big gamble, and we ultimately decided to invest our money elsewhere.

COUNTING THE COST

All too often, we don't calculate the cost before we dive in, and then we wonder why we don't produce a positive return on the investment. Or we didn't realize what we were obligating ourselves to. This is important: if we don't dig for that information in advance, we fail to produce the results. Instead of realizing that and fixing it, we tend to say, "Oh, I don't know. I got busy, and then this thing happened."

If we don't calculate the cost and speculate the return it's going to produce, we're going to make bad decisions. Period. This happens. All the time.

Before we dig too deep here, it's important to acknowledge that not all cost—or return—is monetary. Hard costs are important, but there's also the expense of time and focus lost. You might need to get through a learning curve for a few days or weeks; each of those days is a loss. If you're focused on the offer and not on existing clients, there would be a cost to consider.

Whether your point of value is a seller's guideline, managing a tax protest campaign, or developing a process guide that covers the contract-to-close process, there's a lot of development management involved.

You might have all of the information you need to create that offer of help, but you're also going to need creative assistance in the form of copywriting, design, or task management. You might need an assistant who can organize an event or help with communication. If you try to do it all on your own, you'll be limited to the hours in the day while still trying to respond to customers and go after immediate business.

Another pitfall when we're creating points of value can show up in the details. For example, when a client has been in a home for a while, you might send them neighborhood updates. Let them know what's selling in their neighborhood, which could prompt them to consider selling their own house. If you document the anniversary dates of home purchases for your past clients, you can engage with them as the life cycle on their home shifts. On average, people move every three to seven years. When you reach that time frame, you've got to be in touch with them.

But the more detail you start to add—anniversaries, neighborhoods around each client, personal interests, personal life changes—you have to be able to prioritize. It's not realistic to do everything any more than it's realistic to choose just one "best" thing to do. Intuition can only be a piece of your prioritization.

Even when we prioritize our activities, we usually see about a one in five or one in seven success rate on new points of value. When we build value for future business and future customers, these offers of help often have to be tested and refined, and in order to test and refine them, they have to be feasible, and they have to be executed. If you do little bits of everything or if you haphazardly do things here and there, you'll lower your chances of success. We can't really know whether a point of value will be a hit with customers until it's been in their hands and they're able to react, respond, and evaluate it.

Now, if Garry could have known that Lost Creek—from that cringeworthy story in the last chapter—was going to cost him $76,000 with no ROI, he probably wouldn't have stuck with it so long. Not every single cost can be calculated, but there are plenty that can be. If we really understand these numbers, they can change our approach in small and significant ways alike.

THE VALUE OF POTENTIAL

There's a culture of risk taking among entrepreneurs that's not actually a good one. They're ultimately throwing the dice and gambling—not just with their money, but with their energy and effort. They find themselves committed to all these things without thinking about the cost. If we've put our energy and time into something that we haven't calculated the cost for, there's a high chance that it's not going to happen at all. All that energy and effort just gets flushed down the toilet.

For example, you can work out the value of a market opportunity by counting the number of homes in the market. Then go to the MLS and calculate the turnover rate and average sale price. With those figures in hand, you can look at what market share would produce a specific number of homes sold, and from there you can identify a target volume. How much GCI would you make from that target volume? Would it be worth it?

It's all right if your head is spinning with this kind of math. We've created several ways for you to use these tools in your practice. You can check the website for a tool to calculate this for your own business. You can work it out on your own or plug your data into that tool to work out the target. However you do it, make sure you identify what would be necessary for you to be successful in an area before you go after it.

CALCULATE DEMOGRAPHIC INTEREST

Just as important as calculating your own cost and potential market share, you need to look at the feasibility of an opportunity as well. If the homes in an area fall within a specific price range (usually true of a farm area), you can estimate the income required and the lifestyle needed to afford those homes. In our county in Texas, we can use tax records to pull every bit of demographic data for anybody in a zip code or region to see how it matches up.

We can also tell a lot about the interest a demographic

will have based on the area itself. In the middle of the hill country, there will be one type of interest. Downtown will have another, and East Austin will have its own specific interest. You'll be making some assumptions with this piece, but those assumptions will be pretty well-educated ones based on income levels and desired areas to live in.

You also might wind up with three or four different profiles in an area. In that case, it's more than reasonable to ask people up front, "Do you mind me asking, which of these scenarios fits you best?" This is where you should combine data with listening well and asking good questions of your clients, which we'll get into in the upcoming chapters.

CUSTOMER LIFETIME VALUE

Now we're going to look at the database you likely already have made and then learn to see the value in that list. Then, when you start to use that value calculation as a tool, you can begin to work on your database to make it more robust to provide even more detail.

Because each practice, market, and real estate professional is unique to itself, it's going to take a little bit of speculation and judgment to estimate these values. We've created a calculator for you to work out these estimates, but we can't give you the data to plug into it. It's okay to not be precisely accurate here. The point is to look at your ideas about points of value and determine whether they might be a feasible reality.

To calculate the lifetime value of a client, we're going to use some simple math, demonstrated in the table, that you can easily use with your own data. Of course, we encourage you to calculate your own averages to get a much more accurate baseline to calculate the lifetime value of your clients.

1. Let's assume that your average sales price is $300,000, and your average commission is 3 percent, giving you an average gross commission income of $9,000.
2. Now let's assume your commission split with your brokerage is 80 percent, giving you a take-home of $7,200. Assuming all of these averages, that's the amount you'll take home per sale.
3. We also know from the National Association of Realtors® that, on average, a single client will conduct five real estate transactions, though not necessarily with the same agent.
4. Going a step further, if you do an excellent job with your clients, you have the potential of an average of four referrals from each client. Without a system of staying in touch, however, the average referrals are two per client.
5. Following these numbers, each person represents *five*

of their own transactions, plus *four* referrals with *five* transactions each. That's a potential of *twenty-five transactions* for every client you interact with.

6. Multiply that by your average $7,200 per transaction, and you see that each client represents a potential $180,000 lifetime value.

	Example 1	Example 2	Your Numbers
Your Average Sales Price	$300,000	$235,000	
x Average Commission	3%	2.5%	
Gross Commission Income	$9,000	$5,875	
X Brokerage Split	80%	70%	
x Take Home	$7,200	$4,113	
x 25 Total Transactions	$180,000	$102,813	

EARNING REPEAT AND REFERRAL CLIENTS

According to the NAR, 64 percent of home sellers found their real estate professional because either they worked with the agent before or they got a referral. Just shy of 90 percent of all buyers say they intend to refer their real estate professional after they've bought their home.

Shockingly, in spite of all of these referrals, the typical agent only got 31 percent of their business from repeat or referral business. Somehow, agents are failing to harvest this clear opportunity.

Why is there such a breakdown between the opportunity and its realization? The answer lies in the process. We aren't entitled to repeat and referral business—we have to earn it. Most of us lack a process for nurturing our relationships and cultivating our clients' full lifetime value.

When you have calculated your average lifetime value for your clients, write it on a sticky note and place it somewhere where you will see it regularly. This is the potential that every individual you work with holds. Set it as your screen saver; make it the login for your computer. Use it as a constant reminder of how important it is to maintain a working, productive relationship with every client, every step of the way.

When you start to see just how much potential lies in your interactions with clients, it creates a compelling argument for offering help, staying in touch, and keeping a thorough database. We should be doing everything we can not only to secure that business with the client but to earn their referrals as well.

DON'T GET TRIPPED UP

The biggest obstacle to maximizing this potential and getting new clients is simply ourselves. We don't have an organized CRM (customer relationship management system); we don't have a system to stay in touch consistently; we won't pick up the phone and call people. We don't maximize opportunities with the right tools, tech, or trends. We don't keep the process moving, shaking that dirt down to find the gold.

When we walk all the way back to the first step in this

design process, it's still all about identifying points of value that each of us can personally offer. It's looking internally at what we're good at, what we know, and where our expertise lies to know what we might be currently offering or what we can hone to become an offer. Then it's looking externally and identifying opportunities in the market around us.

How do you know when a market opportunity is right for you? Unfortunately, we can't tell you that. We can't take a one-to-one prescriptive comparison between us and anyone else that tells you exactly what you need to do. And the stakes are high. A large company in a corporate context can afford to see profits go down a bit or to not be as successful. In a small business, these decisions can mean the difference between just surviving and thriving.

With your customer lifetime value number in hand and your database in place, look back at how many transactions you had last year. How many came from repeat or referred business? How much untapped potential is still out there for you? If you aren't tracking this information, now is the time to start. Know where you get your business every year, know where your business should come from, and take the steps necessary to make it happen.

When Garry laid out some specific tasks for Brenda—marketing to her database, using Facebook ads, making phone calls and sending text messages, and going to events—he knew it was going to be uncomfortable for her. He warned her that it'd feel like people didn't want to hear from her, didn't want her emails, and didn't want her messages. She had to remind herself that they did want to hear from her, that she was offering value, and that these were the steps she needed to take to build her business.

She told us, "I'm going to trust you and do whatever I need to, because I'm desperate to build my business." She did, and within the first four weeks she had ten new clients. Just by performing the essential tasks that any entrepreneur needs to do, Brenda more than doubled her sales and reached her goal within three short months.

Imagine that—putting ten new signs in front of ten new homes a month from now. Now, the real question is, what do you imagine you'll do to get there?

SOMETHING TO THINK ABOUT

Have your processes included reaching out to your existing database? Do you even have a database yet? How much potential is your business losing due to languishing contacts?

5

SALES EXPERTISE

No one is born a salesperson. Some folks are more inclined to it, no doubt, but everyone has to learn. Garry today is excellent at that subconscious competence—the air of confidence that only comes from successful sale after successful sale. But it didn't come naturally. He wasn't even trained in it. His background was in business management and operations (with international business expertise, to be specific). That's not sales.

When he fell into real estate, though, he was determined. He quite literally sat at the office doorstep of his mentor, listening for any clues to success he could find. He followed all the advice. He did what successful people said he should do. And one of those things he was told he should do was to knock on doors.

"Go out there and find the neighborhood you want ownership in," they said. "Knock on their door and get in front of them, face-to-face, flesh-to-flesh," they said. Like Brenda from chapter 4, Garry was ready to do anything, so out he went. He identified a neighborhood, hopped into his beat-up Tahoe, and drove over to Barton Creek.

Now, the thing you should know about Barton Creek is that the average sales price for those houses runs around $1.8 million. *Straight to the top, baby,* Garry thought. But actually, the more important thing you should know about Barton Creek is that it's a gated community. It's completely gated with its own private security network.

Gates be damned—we're completely serious here—Garry pulled his car to the side of the road and analyzed his situation. Ultimately, he figured he might not have been born a salesman, but he *was* born tall and athletic. *For such a time as this,* right? The fence was no match for him. He hopped right over in his black suit and set off to knock on some doors.

Garry knew what he wanted to be selling (one day) but had no idea that he wasn't supposed to solicit in a gated, high-value neighborhood. He was told to knock on doors, and so he did.

The person who owned the first house was actually home when he knocked, and Garry confidently told her,

"My name is Garry Creath, and I'm a REALTOR® here. I'm curious—have you guys ever thought about selling your house?"

"No," she said, "but you're trespassing in a no-soliciting neighborhood, and I'm going to call the cops right now." *Slam.*

Now, Garry did what any level-headed, twenty-three-year-old kid would do in this situation: he made a break for it. He took off in an adrenaline-fueled run, hopped the fence a second time, jumped in his car, and sped away.

Now, listen. Successful entrepreneurs don't need to be *born* salespeople, but they *do* need to be competent in sales. And it's not just for selling homes, either. Building a referring relationship with a local business owner requires selling. Hiring and retaining the services of a quality freelancer or employee require constant selling to keep them contributing at optimal levels. So many of our interactions with customers, prospects, partners, employees, and service providers require us to sell solutions, ideas, and services. Yet few of us step into this role with much sales expertise, or, if we do, it's not a skill that we hone over time.

Though there are myriad principles and practices we could cover in this chapter, we're going to stick to just three key, expert-level sales skills that will (hopefully) keep you from running from the cops your first day out.

First, we'll look at mood. Both your mood and your client's mood are an integral part of any sales interaction. Then we'll revisit questions and make sure you're asking the right kinds of thought-provoking ones. Finally, we'll look at principles of persuasion and how you can tie it all together to more effectively communicate your value proposition for each client.

SETTING THE RIGHT MOOD

Pause just for a moment, and think about this: how do you feel right now? There's no wrong answer. How are you feeling? Are you feeling confident? Purposeful, peaceful, excited? Distant, frustrated, overwhelmed? Are you excited or anxious? Think about how you felt before you sat down to read and then how you felt the last time you sat down to read. What was different or similar? Did you absorb the content differently then?

A person's mood, or their emotional state, plays a large role in what they pay attention to, care about, and act on. In sales, mood is the first factor that can become a catalyst or a roadblock.

Picture yourself hosting a gathering for dinner. You've

spent about forty-five minutes preparing a meal, it's 6:30 p.m., and almost everyone has arrived. You're just waiting on one more friend to make it, and then you can sit down to eat and enjoy time together. The phone rings, and because it might be that one friend, you pick it up without even looking at the number. You might even be mid-conversation with the others there, thinking you'll see where your buddy is and then get back to the evening.

But as soon as you pick up, you know. You can hear it. The headset is delayed, the background noise is chatty and obnoxious—the distinct sounds of a call center. The caller is a telemarketer, and they've interrupted your evening to try to sell you something. You don't want to buy anything, certainly not right now. You want to enjoy the evening with your friends and family.

Even though your mood was excellent when they called, what happened to that mood as soon as you realized what they wanted? Even more important, does that person calling you have any chance whatsoever of breaking through? Of course not. A good mood isn't the same as a selling mood, and you were definitely not in a selling mood.

If you're prospecting and calling people you don't know, there's an excellent chance that this scenario will happen to you, though you'll be on the wrong end of the receiver. When you're meeting with clients—even past clients—it's important to pay attention to moods before you launch into an attempt at a sale.

MOOD MATTERS

If you and your client are in the right mood, you'll create a more productive environment for whatever you're trying to accomplish. Real estate especially isn't about just trying to sign this or buy that—you're trying to reach a peak level of productivity together. That requires more than just hard sales.

Garry has a knack for setting moods, and he usually starts with his own. If you aren't sure how to get a handle on your own mood, start with music. The right kind of music can increase endorphins, get you excited, and create a mood that you give off energetically to those around you. We respond to music mentally, emotionally, and even physically. Soothing classical music can help you relax with a glass of wine, or a crooning vocalist might help you reflect. If some familiar rock comes on the radio, you might start reflexively playing the air guitar (Chris does, anyway!). Music has a powerful connection to energy and mood, and you can use it as a tool to create the energy you want when going to meet with a client.

Music is a big part of Garry's routine before meeting with a client, and on one particular occasion, he was pumped up and ready to go as he walked up to the door. But the second he stepped into the room, the weight of the mood was almost palpable. He could tell right away that something was wrong. Rather than forcing his mood on the clients, he simply asked them, "Do you mind if I ask, has something happened overnight that we need to talk about?"

Turns out, the client's mom had died, but they didn't want to change the appointment. Of course, Garry rescheduled. Not only was it the respectful thing to do, but because they weren't in the right mood and mind space to worry about listing and marketing, the meeting wouldn't have been able to accomplish anything.

In addition, Garry's attention to the mood of the room opened the door for a real relationship to be built. He sent flowers to the family, and the client took time to themselves before coming back to work on the sale. When they were ready, they hired Garry, and they continue to refer him today.

SIGNS AND SIGNALS OF MOOD

Early in a relationship, there's not much trust there. You're trying to build a rapport with your clients, but their guard is up. After making sure your own mood is set where it should be, there are some things you can do to clue into their mood and start to work with them in that capacity.

Body language is a great indicator of a person's mood. If their arms or legs are crossed or their body is turned away from you, they're closed off. Watch their facial expressions to see what they're telling you. You can also listen to their tone of voice. Is their inflection monotone or down? What kinds of words are they using?

It's also completely fine to just ask, "Hey, is everything all right?" Checking in shows that you care and are concerned about their well-being—which is a part of taking care of your customers. Ultimately, that's all that sales is, anyway.

If you do check in and they respond with, "Fine," pay attention to the way they say it. It's okay to gently ask, "What does 'fine' mean to you?"

Remember that these signals you're watching for are signals you send as well. By being intentional with your own mood, you can direct the mood of the room and affect your client. Going into a meeting or interaction, Garry likes to go for moods like *powerful, kind, compassionate, curious,* and *open.* You might find your own specific moods that you like to go to. With your mood set and the client in a selling mood, it's time to ask appropriate questions.

ASKING THE RIGHT QUESTIONS

The hallmark sign of a person with effective sales skills is the quality of questions they ask. Are the questions purposefully engineered to provoke a certain kind of response, or do you tend to react and ask questions in the moment? The more you study sales, the more you'll find that designing the right questions in advance, scripting them, and practicing them produces increasingly effective results.

As you begin to ask questions and prepare to listen, keep tabs on the client's mood and controlling your own. If you're working with a client who needs to adjust the price of their home, the mood should be confident. If you go into that scenario with any sort of trepidation, the client will wonder whether you know what you're talking about. Still, that type of confidence should be calm and settled compared to the confidence you'd take to, say, the gym. You can't walk into the meeting pumped up and yelling. That wouldn't go well for anyone. Listen as the conversation progresses and always notice others' responses and reactions to your mood.

In the same vein, keep a calm, even tone. Some activities need a lot of vocal inflection—for example, if you're training your dog. Your inflection's all over the place, and it works. When we speak on stage, we bring a lot of energy and excitement that shows up in our inflection.

But speaking to clients is different. Your voice should always be calm and even, which exudes a confidence that will reflect back to you in returned trust.

LEAD WITH CURIOSITY

Conversations should always begin with curiosity rather than certainty. If you lead with certainty without listening and being curious, it'll feel like you're forcing the other person down a path that you've chosen. Just like watching for their mood, starting with curiosity shows a genuine interest in the client and their life. What's going on in their life? How are they really doing, and how can you help? When the client senses that genuine curiosity, they'll be much more open to working with you.

Lead with curiosity by asking questions. If you can think back through your most recent interactions with clients, how did those conversations go? If you're speaking more than 10 percent of the time, you'll probably want to dial it back a bit. We win when we ask questions and listen, letting our clients talk for 90 percent of the time. That means we're focused on listening to them and extracting the information that we need to continue asking more questions. And that means they'll feel heard.

The key to active listening is that you're listening with the intent to understand, not the intent to respond. When we lead with a mood of curiosity, we're silencing our own inner monologue in order to be curious and understand what they're saying, what's behind it, and what their body language says. We've all got an inner monologue, and often when we're talking with someone, those voices are working up what we can say next. Sometimes, we feel like we have to respond in certain ways in order to sound better or look better or have the answers. But when we do that—when we're just listening for opportunities to respond—we miss out on the real opportunities.

Think about some of the hardest-hitting interviews you've seen on TV. When does the big breakdown come? It's never from an interruption. No one likes to be interrupted. The emotional moments happen when the interviewer says, "Tell me more about that," and then waits. Those silences turn into the most memorable moments, and the interviewer didn't have to say another word.

QUESTIONS TO KEEP IN YOUR ARSENAL

Start a conversation with an open-ended question about something you researched and learned about that person through social media. This is a powerful tool at our disposal. Google them, look them up on Facebook or LinkedIn, and see what's going on in their life right now. Not only will that give you something to talk about, but it can also help you understand what might be directing or charging their mood.

Ask them about their life. "Hey, Chris, I noticed that you've been taking some awesome photos of your kids in your new swimming pool. How was your weekend?"

People are afraid of sounding like they're stalking their clients, but that's not stalking. It's paying attention. Why else would they post something on social media than to share with the people around them? The best way to know that what you've shared has affected someone is for them to bring it up. You're showing them that you care enough to pay attention to them before you try to sell to them.

When the conversation is moving toward what they need and what you might be able to offer, if you don't remember anything else, remember the phrase "Thank you. Can you tell me more about that?" If you always keep that script on the tip of your tongue, you won't have to think about what to say next.

Some other useful, more specific, questions might be "Do you have any concerns about selling your house in today's marketplace?" or "Do you have any concerns about working with me?" It might be tempting to start explaining how great you are, but it's much more pow-

erful to ask an open-ended question and allow them to
lead the conversation.

FIVE WHYS

Open-ended questions keep the conversation moving forward until you've extracted their true concerns. It's like the tactic of asking five whys when necessary. If you were to ask yourself "why," answer it, ask "why" to that answer, and continue this three more times (for a total of five whys), you'd get down to the core and learn a lot about that issue.

For example, if a client says they have to be out by the end of August, don't just take their word for it and start spewing options. Ask, "That sounds important to you. Do you mind if I ask why that date is so critical?" Their answer: they have to be in another house. "Why is that transition at that time so important?" Well, they'll be starting a new school district in September. "Do you mind if I ask why that is so important to you?" We have a special needs child who requires the help of the new school district.— and there it is. Everything you do with that client from there on should drive you forward toward helping them set up the lifestyle they want for their kids. If you know of alternatives to that concern, you can start mitigating them for the client. Maybe you can help them enroll with an intent to move so that the stress of time constraints is removed completely.

The only way you can get to such a specific need and resolution is by listening until you can find the root of their concern. Ask questions, listen with the intent to understand, and then ask further questions to uncover the true motivation behind what they're doing. Then align yourself with them in order to take care of them. This is fundamental to being a master salesperson.

ACTIVE LISTENING

Research shows that a conversation can become uncomfortable after only *four* seconds. Count that out and see how long it actually is. We'll wait—except we don't have to wait long, because four seconds happens fast. You're probably painfully aware of that already, because you know that a conversation can get awkward after the briefest pauses. And what do we do when we get uncomfortable? We fill that silence with words.

Unfortunately for the salesperson, however, we also know that the person who speaks first loses. When we speak just to fill silences or just to respond for the sake of response, our words are often unnecessary. We speak from a place of assumptions and certainty instead of understanding and empathy, and it doesn't usually do us any favors.

You see, the silence isn't just uncomfortable for you, and your head isn't the only one filled with an internal monologue. The client is going through all the same experiences. When you pipe up to break the silence, you're interrupting the monologue in their own head. Part of that internal monologue might be "I wonder whether they're telling the truth" or "I wonder whether this is a good idea." Or it might simply be "Hmmm...interesting." Without paying close attention to their body language, asking thoughtful questions, and taking the time to listen, you really have no idea what they're thinking. And when you talk, you're interrupting that process. They might have just been at the point of deciding to trust you when you interrupt with unnecessary words. We can quickly slip from the brink of trust to "What are they babbling about?"

So as much as we want to avoid interrupting them as they speak, don't interrupt a client's thought patterns, either. If you've come armed with the right preparation and information, their inner monologue will do the selling for you. Listen carefully, and become comfortable in the silence. Put them at ease, and let them know what's going on: "I want you to know that during these silences, I'm listening and documenting what you're saying. I'm trying to listen so I can really hear you and what you need."

YES, AND

Another way to move the conversation forward comes from improv. When participating in improv, you never stop the flow of the performance with a refusal. No matter what's suggested to you, your job is to agree to it and add to it. You are taught to do that by saying "Yes, and..." In this way, you never stifle the other performers' creativity, and you never block up the energy of the performance.

When we're speaking with clients, whether it's someone brand new or a previous client who's not quite happy about something, there's no reason to say "no." We should never put our clients in a position of defensiveness. If they have a suggestion that's completely unreasonable, take the improv route. If Chris were to offer tequila first thing in the morning, Garry might say, "Yes, I do enjoy tequila. And what I'd really love is a cup of coffee."

Try adding this to your next conversations with a client, and see where it takes you: "Yes, I see why that's a good idea. And what I know works especially well is..."

LISTEN WITHOUT RESPONSE

Truly patient, active listening is such an unfamiliar experience that it can feel quite intense. Try this exercise: Find a coworker, client, or spouse, and sit knee-to-knee with them. Put your hands on your knees, look them straight in the eye, and ask them to tell you five things about you that they love. Don't respond at all. Keep the same posture and just listen. Feel what it is to listen without response.

Now sit with the same posture, knee-to-knee, and ask them to tell you five things they *don't* like about you. This can get really heavy, so it's okay to ask them to keep it light and make things up. Maybe they talk about your shirt or your hair. All the while, you're just going to sit. Feel your body being perturbed. Sit with the discomfort. As they tell you each thing, look them in the eyes and simply say, "Thank you."

When you're listening to clients with that same intensity—responding even to criticism with "Thank you" and "I can see why you might say that. Can you tell me more?"—they're left with nowhere to go. Any defensiveness is completely diffused. This goes hand in hand with leading with curiosity, and it moves the conversation toward resolution rather than firing back.

GET COMFORTABLE BEING UNCOMFORTABLE

Silence is uncomfortable. It just is. And it's human tendency to want to get out of tension as quickly as possible. We want to escape it. But business isn't a black-or-white thing. You don't get to be stressed or calm, uncomfortable or at ease. It's okay to be in a place of tension, and that's a skill that we all have to develop.

If you have a muscle area that you want to develop, you have to put that muscle into tension. You have to work it and stretch it in ways you don't normally. That's the sort of tension we need to work on from a business philosophy standpoint, too. If you're reading this book to stretch beyond your comfort levels as a real estate professional to realize your role as an entrepreneur, you're probably already becoming familiar with tension. Now it's time to expand the tension you can carry, in order to continue to innovate.

If you're not in a place of discomfort in some way on a regular basis, consider whether you're striving to grow. Could that be why you've felt stagnant? We've noticed that the times we feel too comfortable are the times we have to reexamine where we are and what we need to do to change. Our life goals should not be to be comfortable. The goal is to continue to grow as a person and as an entrepreneur, and that means becoming comfortable being uncomfortable. Silence is a good place to start.

BUILD TRUST BEFORE PERSUASION

People rarely research all of their options to make a thoughtful decision. Instead, we look to shortcuts that will help us save time and energy. Robert Cialdini—author of *Influence,* the classic book on persuasive principles— identified six universal shortcuts that guide our behavior. These include reciprocity, scarcity, authority, consistency, likeability, and consensus.

Listening and being attuned to mood is interwoven in these principles—establishing likeability, and often authority and consistency as well. The respect you give to clients as you listen intently can lead to reciprocal trust and listening on their part, as well.

The great thing about the kind of sales we're making is that it's not about a specific product that you're trying to push on people. We're selling the idea that we are best suited to help them reach their goals. In that light, persuasion is simply expressed in being an excellent helper.

A true salesperson doesn't always offer what they have but also what other people can provide to take care of the client's concerns. Even though you aren't a plumber or a mover, when you provide access to resources that will solve those problems, you're providing the offer of help. Listen to the concerns of other human beings and then make an offer of help without any further agenda. Incidentally, this will build trust and rapport that contribute to persuasion later on.

SOMETHING TO THINK ABOUT

How might you apply these techniques to the following scenarios: while talking on the phone with a prospect, during your listing appointment, and while showing properties to a buyer?

6

MARKETING PRINCIPLES

As an entrepreneur and a businessperson, you have a million and one distractions that will show up as potential marketing advantages. Back in the day, for real estate, the talking sign was all the rage. Then there was the automated fax messaging sales assistant. Then CRMs and email marketing and Facebook and Google and—there always has been and always will be someone promising better sales through some kind of marketing advantage. Some of these technologies, tools, and techniques are valid. Most are not. In order to avoid getting caught up in the distractions, we have to learn some basics.

You don't have to become a marketing expert or be fluent in all of the latest strategies. But when you understand marketing principles and fundamentals, you can evaluate each technique, tool, and strategy to determine whether it fits within the bigger picture of your business. The fundamentals allow us to evaluate what's working and—more importantly—*not* working within our business. It's a diagnostic tool. In fact, when an expert can look at a marketing campaign and see what's not working, it's because they have a handle on the fundamentals, not because of what they know about techniques.

Let's step outside of the context of marketing for a second and back into blueprints and construction. If you were a general contractor and noticed that one of your contractors started showing up with new tools, you'd probably do some pretty thorough research. You'd want to know that those tools weren't going to do any damage. You'd want them insured as special equipment. You'd want a good handle on the positive effects. And, if the tools were really good, you'd want all of your contractors to start using them, too.

If, on the other hand, you were to ignore the tools entirely, you'd be open to a number of potential consequences. What if the tools were to make a person slower? Or it introduced a new element of risk that ultimately got you sued when someone got hurt before you were insured properly? Even if that contractor's role is more technical than your own expertise, you're going to have enough of an understanding of the fundamentals to know how to avoid these negative outcomes and keep the project on track.

Now, there is a learning curve associated with any marketing advantage. When you're a solo entrepreneur, that means you have to commit to learning how to use the technologies and strategies you decide to use. Until you move from working on your own to hiring contractors, staff, or experts to do it, you'll need to learn it yourself. That does require a commitment and an effort beyond a basic understanding.

Regardless of who is implementing your marketing strategy, we've found that it all comes down to this: When marketing works, it's because of one simple principle. When marketing fails, it's because there's a breakdown in one or more elements of that principle. The fundamental principle to follow is this: effective marketing speaks to the right person, using the right message, at the right time.

It doesn't matter whether you're running an ad on Google or Facebook, sending out an email, or putting a classified ad in the newspaper—it all comes down to this fundamental principle. As any sort of entrepreneur or business owner, if you don't go for the right person with the right message at the right time, you'll pay the price. Of course, the actual price of marketing is changing drastically.

Garry used to spend $500 to get postcards in front of 500 people only to have no idea what happened with any of them. Not so anymore. You can spend $50 to get in front of hundreds or thousands of people, and everything is trackable. But a failed marketing strategy comes with a cost all its own, and that can usually be prevented at the onset by keeping an eye on these principles.

We're going to start by getting you comfortable with that fundamental strategy in this chapter, and then we'll move on to some important tactical skills in chapter 8. That's the chapter you've been itching to read, we know, but hang with us. Let's first make sure you have a solid strategy that will get your campaign in front of the right people, with the right message, at the right time.

GET IN FRONT OF THE RIGHT PERSON

Too often, marketing pieces are not created with a specific person in mind. If your offer of help isn't designed for a specific person, you'll never help who you need to. Your marketing efforts should be crafted with the same intentionality. Any marketing campaign, activity, or collateral should be designed with a specific intended audience in mind.

Think about two different (broad) markets that you might reach out to for real estate purchases: home buyers and real estate investors. They'll each have very different priorities.

Even looking at the same home, these two people will be thinking different thoughts. Home buyers will be primarily thinking of livability and their future in the home, while investors will be looking for an income-producing future. Buyers are thinking about moving in; investors are thinking about cost of repair and time to market. The home buyer is thinking about colors to paint the home to bring life and their personality to it, and the investor is thinking painting neutral colors that will appeal to tenants or buyers.

Based on your current marketing objectives, you might have many audiences. Whenever you make it to a one-on-one sales conversation with an individual, you've obviously found the right person. But the benefit of marketing is that you get a one-to-many approach. The right person can be found in a number of audiences—your message will never be for a single individual.

Your audience—and the right person—might broadly be prospective home buyers, sellers, and past clients. For each of those, you might have a specific kind of buyer or seller in mind, and for each of those you'll need to craft a message that applies to them specifically and seeks to reach them at the right time in their lives.

DISCOVER YOUR CUSTOMER PROFILE

We've worked through this over the years, and we've got a set of questions for you to use to discover your customer's profile. Whenever you have a marketing campaign, wrestle through these questions for each audience that you want to reach. Most breakdowns happen at this point, so take your time, every time.

The questions are these: Who are they? What are their problems? What have they recently bought? What did they like or dislike about that process? And what are their biggest fears, concerns, and desires?

Who Are They?

This is a simple question of demographics—age, location, gender, income, etc. Depending on the technology you're using, you can break it down even further, such as whether they have children.

This one question alone won't unlock the secrets of the right message or point you directly to the right person, but it'll give you a good start. The point of this question is to start thinking about their perspective.

If you're farming a certain area, buyer concerns for every single listing will be very different. Each demographic factor gives you some insight into individual characteristics that will shape buyer concerns.

What Are Their Problems?

As an individual, a couple, a family, a demographic—what problems are they facing? Does your product or service solve those problems? This is a big one. It's encompassed in the problem we all face when pricing a home: it doesn't matter what we think the home is worth; the only number that matters is what the buyer will pay. It doesn't matter what excellent product or offer of help you have—if it doesn't solve the right person's problem, they won't want it anyway.

Getting into the problems that a buyer has is getting into their psychology. For example, if someone is pursuing new opportunities, they're probably solving the problem that *they're flat broke*. We're all driven by problems—we all have a problem we want to solve. When we know what problem our buyer wants to solve, we can start to think like them. You have to understand their problems in order to communicate with them.

What Have They Recently Bought?

We spend our time and money on what's most important

to us. You might say eating healthy is a priority to you but spend all your money at McDonald's. Now, it doesn't matter whether you eat there five times a day—that's your prerogative. But if you're saying you're interested in healthy foods, we can look at your recent purchases and know that either you're not the right person or we don't have the right message.

Purchase history is another layer into client psychology. How many times have you seen a buyer purchase a car right before they try to finance a house? With all those lending hoops, that's just not good timing. What are they thinking when they do that? Are they feeling like they're making progress? Is it about prestige?

One of our clients recently purchased a Bentley. From that purchase, we know that their vehicle is a concern of theirs. That new house they're buying will need a nice garage for that new Bentley. It'll need to be on a certain side of town, no matter how beautiful it is, in order to satisfy their need for prestige. Purchase history can shape what you know about a person, beyond what they'll simply tell you.

What Did They Like or Dislike about Their Purchase?

Sales training for one-on-one situations will tell you that people think of their recent purchase as not just the product but also whether the experience was positive or negative. So when they bought that car, how did it go? Was it positive or negative, and why?

Maybe they purchased real estate from someone they didn't like. The first question you should ask them is *why*. You want to know why their experience was problematic so that you can avoid offering a similar experience. If we don't think about the buyer's recent experiences, there is a chance we then inadvertently present them with the exact thing they were moving away from. And right to their faces!

What Are Their Biggest Fears, Concerns, and Desires?

If you can get to this point of understanding with your marketing campaign, you'll hit the jackpot. When you get inside the head of the client who owns a Bentley, hitting their desire for prestige, you'll attract more customers like them.

It will affect your entire presentation, because it's about identity as much as the product. Who they're buying from and associating with is important. They need someone who's their equal. They won't be caught referring a nobody. So if you're going to market to people who have Bentleys, part of the message has to be about who you are and the identity that you have. It's credibility, and it matters.

CONVEY THE RIGHT MESSAGE

All of the information you've gathered and investigated in identifying the right person can now start to shape the right message. This represents the value or concept that you want your audience to accept, and it speaks directly to what your customers and prospects care about.

You should also know that it's rare to get the message right the first time, and that's okay. We have to discover the right message for an audience. Keep trying. When the right person's interests are well defined, it's possible to design a better message for them.

Let's say we've defined the right person for our campaign as any past clients who've owned a home for three years or more, which means they probably have some equity built up. We might specifically zero in on those who are interested in future security in retirement and still have a long time before it happens. We might even be able to estimate an income range for those clients.

With this profile in mind, we can design a specific message for that person about real estate investing. This will be a far different message than for someone who is a seasoned real estate investor that's not part of our network. The message should reflect that difference.

ADDRESS THEIR UNDERLYING NEEDS

All of the information gathered to identify the right person can help inform the right message. Maybe they purchased a home organization system, trying to make more space in their apartment by organizing. What might your message be to get in front of them? *Reorganizing your closet isn't going to be enough!* To catch them at the right time, you might even place your message where people shop for home organization products.

You might also find that when they made that home organization purchase, they liked looking at lots of options. They didn't like feeling manipulated by a sales consultant. This is especially common when comparing millennials and younger generations with older generations. Before, people sought out help when making a purchase. But younger generations like to get educated first so that they already have some knowledge whenever they do talk to someone.

These sensitivities make active listening that much more important. Listen to their concerns and what they didn't like about recent purchases, but also listen to what they're not directly saying. You might find an inner drive—for example, "My kids should grow up in a real home" might mean, "I grew up in a home, and my friends have homes and their kids live in a home."

They might be saying one thing, but indicating their real concerns in other ways. Maybe it's their peer group, their concern with school districts, and so on. Using questions and listening closely to both what they're saying and what they're revealing unintentionally can shape your marketing for the better. We all have triggers operating at a subconscious level.

Most of our purchasing decisions are satisfying one of ten needs. Even when you're making rational and logical decisions to purchase something simple, like a financial instrument to save or invest money, the real reason behind the purchase isn't just your investments—it's going to be a deeper trigger point.

TEN TRIGGERS FOR BASIC HUMAN DESIRES

1. Money and a Better Job	6. Social Advancement
2. Security in Old Age	7. Improved Appearance
3. Popularity	8. Personal Prestige
4. Praise from Others	9. Better Health
5. More Comfort	10. Increased Enjoyment

Each of these basic needs—money, security, praise, social advancement—operate on a subconscious level as true, if not hidden, motivation. When you talk to your right person or consider things from their perspective, which of these needs are they trying to fulfill?

DON'T ASSUME

So what does your "right person" actually need? You can't just craft a message around demographics or generalized concerns. All of the questions you've asked so far have to stack up on each other. Starting with demographics, you can ask the next questions the right way.

If they've got two kids and are college educated, they'll have concerns about their kids going to college, which means their income level will be an issue. Then there can be any number of problems when it comes to real estate. They might be tired of renting an apartment, or they might want to live somewhere with better schools. They might still carry student loans from their own education.

The catch is that, as humans, we like to think we know what somebody wants. Chris has a habit of thinking he knows exactly what his wife wants, for example (a mistake many spouses make, we think). She'll have a challenge, and Chris will respond by telling her she should do exactly XYZ.

How often have you been in that position? You could have sworn that's what they wanted. It's a pretty human dynamic to assume. You care about that person and think you're approaching it from their point of view. The problem is that you're approaching it from your own point of view. You have to do some work to get into their perspective and learn how to meet them where they are.

So don't just make stuff up. Talk to previous clients, current clients, and prospective clients. Get back to the questions and active listening that we've practiced in previous chapters and use that to inform your marketing activity.

ASK THE RIGHT QUESTIONS

In any marketing conversation, when someone is seriously considering your product or service, they're going to ask themselves, "Why this person?" The answer to this question should already be clear from a marketing perspective. You don't want this to happen late in the process, where they have to discover or figure out the advantage that you bring to the table. Part of your message needs to be points of advantage, and you need to incorporate that into your marketing plan.

The best way to discover your clear points of advantage is to—surprise, surprise—ask! You can go back to all of your past clients, if you'd like. It's extremely beneficial information. During the process with a new client, ask them if they're interviewing any other agents. After you sign the agreement with them, ask what made you stand out. Why did they choose you? When you know what works, replicate it! If you can share that advantage with everyone to help them make that decision in the first place, your marketing will be powerful.

Even when you're excelling and outcompeting those around you, there's always room for improvement. You can get that point of attraction, but to get people to continue, you have to know what they want. Have they liked something specific about working with you or the firm? That's a new advantage to add.

When you ask a customer what they like most, they might not say it was the way that you marketed properties online, even if that's why they started with you. Maybe, after they worked with you through a buying and selling process, they most enjoyed the weekly updates that helped them know what was going on. As always, active listening is vital in order to catch those clues toward moments of value. Your message might not include everything your people have suggested, but that information to start to design a better option.

Finally, make sure you're always striving toward a more effective design for future customers. Ultimately, your offer is simply, "You should work with me," but competition is constantly evolving. The right message is where we create the *why*, and that's why we have to constantly improve it.

REACH THEM AT THE RIGHT TIME

Although social media marketing has much to say about times of day, that's not really what we're going for with reaching our right person with the right message at the right time. Here, it's the context that matters. What exactly are they doing at that moment in time? Is it a good time for them to respond to your call to action? Are you just going for an impression?

Think about a billboard. Just about all billboards grab some kind of attention. But then there are the ones that say, "Would you like to increase your business by 175,000 percent?! That's what I did and you can too! Email us now at increasemybusiness@45137increase-mybusiness.com or text 45137 BUSINESS to 11347 NOW!"

Even the person stuck in traffic staring at that billboard isn't going to get it. (Which, honestly, is probably a fundamental error with all three of these principles. We're not sure who that right person for a billboard like that would be, but that's definitely not the right time or message.)

Now, however, think what might happen if nature calls while you're on that same stretch of road, and you see a great big sign that says "Pull Over! Clean Restrooms This Exit!" That's a clear message, providing tremendous value, that gave you a specific call to action right when you were ready to take it. It was the right context for that message, and you were exactly the right person for it.

The good news is that if your right person has found you online, they're in one of two modes: searching or consuming. Both are promising. All too often, however, we ignore their specific context. We add in "text now" or "click now" without thinking about what they're actually doing *right now*. What's the likelihood of them actually texting or emailing or clicking an ad link now? If there's no call to action, are they going to make it back to you at all? If that billboard said, "Pull over in five miles" and there are three exits in between, you'll forget about the ad and pull into another gas station. In light of who they are as the right person and what message they need that conveys your value to them, what is their context and how does your marketing campaign fit into it?

The right time is when your audience is able to receive your message, is searching for something your message offers, and can act on that message. If you're marketing real estate on Facebook, the right person might be someone in the market to buy a home; the right message could be pretty pictures of homes you have listed; and the right context could be in their newsfeed in the evenings while they are just browsing, with a "tap here for more information" button. Then, when they make it to the landing page with easily scheduled showings, it will be an appropriate and reasonable call to action *and* offer of value.

APPLY THIS TO YOUR OWN PRACTICE

People often mistake advertising for something that it's not. Or at least something it doesn't have to be. They'll say, "I don't like advertising. I don't even like having ads shown to me." But that's only true for ads that don't provide value. They haven't taken into consideration who you are and what you want and need. They haven't thought about the message you want to see or the time and context you want to see it in.

If you don't care about basket weaving, an ad about it will feel like spam. But if you're in the grocery store after work, thinking about a quick and easy meal you can make before you get home, a kiosk or pick-up dinner offer will serve a good purpose. There's value in it for you.

Nobody likes advertising—until it's focused on providing the value you're looking for. Every time you craft a marketing campaign, look at the image containing your message, consider the people you want to reach, and ask yourself whether it's the right time. Picture yourself as this customer.

Think about it in these terms completely removed from

real estate. If you're at the beach, maybe feeling a little parched or tired, what might be relevant to you? A suntan booth will probably not cut it. It's going to take a cold drink and some food. The person who's walking away from a whole day of surfing will have a different set of priorities than someone who has been inside reading all day.

Your client might not be terribly concerned with what their house is worth. That's all right. That's how you want to think about marketing. When we try to force it onto the wrong context, all we're doing is setting up a negative judgment about ourselves. It's so important to think about each of these factors—right person, right message, right time—or we risk our message coming across as offensive or pushy. Consumers put blinders on now, and when you put your message in front of them, all of the right factors need to be in play or they won't even look.

Right person, right message, right time should be evaluated for every single marketing effort you put into place. We don't even blend messaging for people who are selling their home to buy a home. Their concerns while selling are different than their concerns for buying, so we go through the selling process and then the buying process separately. Think about all of your campaigns, emails, mailers, and offers of value as separate messages. Who is the right person, each time? What is their context?

To put this into practice right now, pull out a marketing piece that you've done recently. It could be an email that you sent out to clients, an advertisement you ran in the newspaper or on Facebook, or a post on social media that you hoped might generate business. Find one, and run it through the principles of right person, right message, right time. Use it as a diagnostic tool.

- **Right Person:** Who was the right person for that advertisement? How would you describe them? What criteria do they have? Now, what criteria of person were you hoping would see this ad? Is that criteria specific enough? (Hint: "anyone who wants to buy a home in Austin" is too broad.) What areas of improvement could have gotten your ad to the right person?
- **Right Message:** Assuming the right person, how well did the message line up with the person you needed to reach? Was the message reasonable or coherent for that person? What improvements could be made to better speak to who they are and what they need? Remember that the message includes every component of the ad, from headline to call to action to images to overall essence. What is associated with that message, and will it ultimately appeal to the right person?
- **Right Time:** What was the context for this ad or marketing piece? What was the recipient doing when they saw it? Is the message asking for something reason-

able given the time and context? How could the time and context have been improved?

Now, when one of these pieces is missing, you really can't answer for the other two. If you don't have the right person identified, it doesn't matter what the message is. Or if you hit the right person at the right time with a bad message, you've missed an opportunity. Take the time to work through each step, and you'll be able to assess your marketing strategy and come up with ways to improve it.

No one else can answer these questions for you. No one can set up your marketing campaign from a generalized template—not a successful, sustainable campaign, anyway. We all have our own audiences that we attract and serve and take care of. Work through these questions for yourself, your market, and your strengths in order to distinguish your own right person, right message, and right time.

SOMETHING TO THINK ABOUT

Think about all of your outreach and interactions with potential, current, or past clients—emails, calls, mailers, or anything. Where could you apply marketing principles to improve these interactions?

7

BUILDING A MARKETING CAMPAIGN

Napoleon Hill tells the story of gold miners who worked and worked a plot of land, looking for gold back in the days of the forty-niners. Try as they might, they kept coming up empty. Finally, they decided their equipment would be worth more than continued wasted efforts, so they sold off their gold-mining gear and then packed up and left. When the next person came in, equipment in hand, they dug and mined for just three feet more before—you guessed it—striking gold.

Paulo Coelho's alchemist learns a similar lesson. He travels the world in pursuit of treasure, but when he finally finds what he's looking for, it's in his own backyard.

This is a story that humans have recycled and retold in various forms for generations, because it's a lesson we all need to learn. In the early days of Facebook advertising, we were working with it even before "boost post" was available as an option. The goal was to market a workshop, so the Facebook ad promoted the workshop and took people to a landing page. Chris set the budget for $1,200 and hit start. About $500-$600 in, Chris decided Facebook just didn't work for him. People were clicking, but it wasn't producing results. Nothing was happening to create an ROI, so he wrote off the tool completely.

Here's what's significant about that little anecdote: That's Chris's job. He *does* marketing. He *is* marketing. And it was still his inclination to throw his hands in the air and walk away.

We're all susceptible to that frustration. It happens. It's easy to get excited about a new tool or technology but, in that excitement, overlook the fundamental discipline of planning effectively, testing, and improving upon it.

It's okay to jump into the execution of a campaign for the purposes of learning the basics, but if you really want to limit the time it takes to put together a quality campaign that gets results, you've got to think about the details. When you take the time to plan out your marketing campaigns in the right person, right message, right time format, marketing compliance and conversion almost certainly go up.

The biggest rookie mistake we see in marketing is rushing into building the creative elements without asking fundamental questions about the profile of the person whom the marketing is created for, what they care about, and what message will provide value and elicit a response.

There's huge benefit in marketing online, because people are looking for what you have to offer. They're ready. And we have many tools available to us, from social media to pay-per-click to content on landing pages and websites. You can even use real estate search sites to create an identity for yourself. But there's also a massive pitfall.

In this chapter, we're assuming you have your marketing principles from chapter 6 in place and are ready to start strategizing and using those tools that you might have written off in the past. As an entrepreneur, some of these marketing skills are more important than others, but depending on your scenario, you might be doing the marketing yourself. We're going to focus on strategic marketing skills, both so you can understand what's happening as the entrepreneur and so you can function in marketing if you have to go it alone.

SETTING REALISTIC EXPECTATIONS

Far too often, we walk into marketing strategies and campaigns with a false set of assumptions. We start using tech or strategy assuming that we already know how to make it successful—often without any education, guidance, coaching, or support. We're blindly operating a system, hoping it will work.

Then, like Chris and his Facebook ads, we assume the tech didn't work. Rather than blame ourselves for not getting the right education, we pin it on a fault with the email platform, social media, Facebook, Google—the list is endless. To make the most of these incredible tools at your disposal, you have to commit to figuring out how to make it work.

Because here's the thing: large firms and marketing organizations are just as lost as you are. The only difference is that they have a big budget and lose a lot more money in the process of seeing their "results."

Think about what it'd be like if you'd never seen an airplane. If you had no idea what it was used for, you'd have no idea how to get into the sky. You wouldn't know what it was at all. You've got to get the right education in order to know its purpose and what to do with it.

Or, to make things more personal, as real estate professionals we're familiar with houses in general but wouldn't know how to build a really sturdy one. It'd take tools, education, and apprenticing. That's the approach we need to take with marketing. If you can learn to use it well, it will produce amazing results, but like everything else, it takes time.

KEY TERMS

- **Marketing Activity:** This is any task producing a marketing outcome. Posting on social media, sending an email, and mailing a postcard are examples of marketing activities.

- **Marketing Campaign:** This is any series of marketing activities constructed together to achieve a common set of objectives, such as recruiting home sellers or staying in touch with your database.

- **Marketing Plan:** This is a sequence of marketing campaigns that you intend to implement over period of time.

It's also important to remember that all of these tools are predicated on the right person, right message, right time principle. The right person will be different at different times, and it is historically difficult to connect with them. We often don't take the time to try—as evidenced by things like tattoo removal ads coming up when you don't have any tattoos to begin with.

When you have the right person, get the right message— which will probably not be the message you would have crafted for yourself. From a demographics standpoint, we might think like our customers. But from a priority standpoint, it's just not true. A house in the best school district, walking distance from the school, would have great appeal to a certain buyer, but if your kids are in college that won't be your priority. Just like what we think our homes are worth isn't important when we're the sellers—it's what the buyer thinks that counts.

This matters for marketing because something related to someone's current problem will get their attention. Think about what happens when you've got a pressing problem. You might lose some sleep. You have a hard time focusing. It's an open loop that you can't solve, so it's always right on the surface of your consciousness.

Finally, if you have the right person and right message but it's not time for them to consume it or act on it, it won't work. They might see your message on the billboard but think it's not the right time. They might have purchased their home six months ago, which means they're not in the market. It takes all three factors to create a successful marketing campaign.

WORKING TOWARD THE BEST APPROACH

Like the gold miners or the alchemist giving up too soon, it's all too common to run campaigns or create collateral, experience a failure, and then assess the campaign or collateral as ineffective. After Chris decided that "Face-book ads don't work," he read a blog post about someone who was having great success with the same exact tool. Chris had just given up too early on it. And, if we're being honest, he simply didn't know what he was doing.

When he tested a similar campaign after learning a bit, lo and behold, results were much better. He hadn't known how to use the tool to reach the right person with the right message, so he committed time and energy into learning how to use the marketing tool. And now he uses it with great success.

On the other side of things, we've also seen far too many people neglect to take the initiative when it comes to trying new marketing tools and technology, and that's unfortunate. When we see new marketing tools work, it's the decision maker who drives the machine, who pushes their team to try this new service, try this tool, try this platform. The people doing the everyday mechanics of marketing often won't try to push the envelope. We haven't quite figured out why that is—we just know it's a thing, and it's a thing that you can stop within your practice.

TEST AND TEST AGAIN

Even now that we know how to use our marketing tools better, we still take the time to test our campaigns, collateral, audience selection criteria, different messages, and different placements or formats to figure out how to make the campaign work for the right person.

In fact, although we set up our entire year of marketing at an annual retreat, it winds up getting revised on a monthly basis. We look at it once a week to keep an eye on marketing activity, because there's so much going on. You've got to constantly look back and see what worked, what didn't work, and what needs to improve to increase effectiveness.

Apply a "test and improve" mentality to your marketing strategy rather than hoping for "one-hit wonders." There is no mountaintop moment where you sit down and decide you've made it and know what you're going to do from here on in. It's a discipline—constantly thinking about the future and reflecting on the results of the past and then updating your plans accordingly.

Some things that we test regularly include the following:

- New audience selection criteria
- Whether income range is better than net worth
- Whether a video or multi-image ad works better

As you test your campaign or collateral, ask a few questions about the results in order to develop new tests and to improve your marketing. If we were to run a Facebook ad specifically for database collection on real estate investments that emphasize ROI and didn't get a lot of response, we might change "ROI" to "real estate investment 101" to see whether that worked better. Or, with the same campaign, we might see whether a single image worked okay or try a short video about the concepts to see whether that performed better.

The important thing is to keep the right mindset as you test. You can't just give up when it looks like something didn't work. Improve the approach and try again. You might send out a postcard once and then decide it didn't work. Why? Because no one called you? That's not a sufficient test in the first place. Maybe you weren't measuring it at all. Maybe you weren't looking at various points of effectiveness. Maybe you could have taken a second shot at it to see whether a different approach would work better.

When that first Facebook ad campaign "didn't work," Chris didn't configure it right. But he approached it with a buy or die mentality: "Well, they're either going to buy the program or they're not." That's not a sufficient test. It wasn't until later that he learned to deploy testing and improve his approach within Facebook.

TAKING THE RIGHT CHANCES

Tools can give us a great advantage as entrepreneurs. They allow us to add capability and capacity without any additional effort. Although you might need to expend some money in the beginning to acquire the tool and develop the skill to use it, you'll make up the cost quickly. After that, the cost for ongoing use is usually low. They can also give you quite an edge.

On the other hand, when you go to a real estate conference, those trade show floors are full of shiny pennies. They all have something that claims you should buy and implement it, and if you close just one deal in a year it will pay for itself. (*But wait! There's more!*) Real estate entrepreneurs are also a market, and companies love to market their products to us. There are endless services and products to help us. We go in all excited and pick up that shiny penny, shelling out a lot of money in the process. But the problem is that there's more than just the initial financial cost. There's also the time and energy required trying to understand and then implement it.

When we started using Facebook ads—really using them, after Chris jumped back in—no one else was doing it. We got lots of great campaign results because it gave us an edge on our competitors. Now we're looking at Instagram, YouTube, and other platforms that give a new competitive advantage. When you look at a tool and evaluate a technology, look for the advantage that you can gain from it and the cost to acquire that advantage.

In any case, there are tools that are essential for marketing. Using your personal email to send out marketing messages to large groups of people is terribly inefficient compared to broadcasted messages on a marketing email provider that will report on campaign progress and effectiveness.

Tools come with a cost, yet we often overlook and underestimate the cost to acquire the skill to use that tool. We look to the tool to solve the problem, not realizing it requires our own effort to make it work. As a practice, we have to spend time researching marketing tools, understanding the capabilities and capacity they offer, and then calculating the cost of both the tool and the skills you'll need to use it.

Just like when you looked at points of value and calculated their benefit and cost, you've got to do the same with marketing tools and technologies. Dive deeper so that when someone tells you, "I've got this great marketing tool for only $25 a month, and all you need is one deal in ten years to pay for it," and you find out with extra research that it'll take about 2,000 hours to learn how to use it, you can then walk away and find something better.

PROCESS FOR CRAFTING A POWERFUL BRAND

BUILDING A CAMPAIGN

To put all of this into action, let's walk through a seven-step process for building a well-designed marketing campaign. Our goal is to use these campaigns to *assist* in tasks such as brand building, promoting your local presence, collecting repeat and referral business, and generating leads. Remember that using marketing alone is not as powerful as having a well-rounded practice, and that sometimes your marketing campaign will only do one or two of those things, and that's okay. It just depends on your objectives and the thoughtfulness of your design.

We're going to use a specific example of a campaign we have in the works right now in order to show you how to implement it—and it is still in process. This isn't a prescription for a campaign to copy but rather a demonstration of a process that you can apply to every marketing objective you create in your own practice.

Now, most of our marketing campaigns are missing some key ingredients for generating good results. If you haven't started with the right person, right message, right time building block principles of good marketing, you won't be able to build a good campaign. Likewise, even if you have the principles down and have been cautious about the way your message is crafted, skipping some of these steps can make your overall strategy falter.

SET GOALS

This might seem like common sense, but unless you clearly define your goals and objectives, you likely won't achieve anything. This is deeper than *more leads, more sales, more income.* It's easy to slip into vague goals and objectives. But if you don't get specific about what you want to accomplish with a campaign, the likelihood that you will achieve those goals will significantly diminish. *Increase business* isn't likely to happen, because it's not clear what you actually want.

In order to set clear goals and objectives, write down what you want the campaign to achieve. Take note of any units of measurement that can gauge progress toward those objectives. Both of these questions will drive you toward a concrete goal instead of vague hopes. The more specific you can be, the more likely it is that you won't be disappointed.

Even now, we wind up with campaigns that aren't really specific. It's not like veterans are immune from this—we run into a campaign and set it up without thinking about it, and then realize after the fact that the results reflect that lack of care. Ask yourself what criteria you're going to use to determine whether the campaign is a success so that at the end of the campaign you don't feel like you've wasted time, energy, and effort.

Finally, ask yourself what you want to learn from the campaign. Often, we hope and think we'll just run a campaign that will generate a bunch of leads. But we have to learn how to do the things that will accomplish that objective in the first place, and we can always learn something from the data and experience of a marketing campaign that can help us in the future.

Let's look at our campaign in the works. The goal is to acquire ultra-high-end listings in our specific market. In order to do that, we have to increase the quantity of conversations we're having with the owners of those listings. Marketing can only take us so far—marketing can't close. So in order to get to those listings, the real goal for the marketing campaign is to increase the conversations that might possibly lead to the listings.

To gauge progress, we can certainly measure the listings, but if we only measure the results and not the steps along the way, we'll miss any areas of breakdown. So we look at the number of listing appointments, the number of initial consultations, and the number of conversations initiated in the first place. How many people respond to this campaign at the start of this pipeline? This campaign can be considered successful if we're starting people in the pipeline with conversations initiated, and extra successful if we're acquiring listings. After the campaign runs for a little bit, we can get some numbers under our belts to better gauge how many conversations or listings can be considered a success.

Because we've never done this campaign before, what we want to learn from it is simple: we need to figure out what offer of value will entice those listings. What do we need to offer to get high-end homeowners' attention and provoke action? What content and sequence of information do we need to follow? What medium do we need to follow, and what do we need to say and offer?

If you don't set solid expectations—not only for the final results but also for the steps along the way—you'll be disappointed. If our only criteria is a commission check in the bank, without any steps or timeline, we're talking about nine to twelve months from the time the marketing campaign starts to the time the results happen. If we don't set appropriate expectations about what a campaign is supposed to do, we'll give up too early.

Even recently, with LinkedIn's new ad features, it's easy to jump in and play around without any objectives, which then doesn't produce the results we want, and thus decide LinkedIn must not work for us. There's a place for experimenting for potential, but as soon as you've passed that stage and are looking to progress in your experience and objectives, you have to get more specific. Get clear on those objectives, criteria, and what you want to learn, and you'll create a better investment of time, energy, and money.

SPECIFY YOUR AUDIENCE

Yep, we're back to right person, right message, right time. For every campaign that you build, you've got to identify the specific audience that you want to reach. Who is the target audience for your campaign, and what criteria will you use to specify that audience? What assumptions are you making about that audience?

For our in-progress campaign, our objective is ultra-high-end listings for a specific area of Austin, making our audience the owners of Austin's luxury and high-end homes who might want to sell. You might say that's sufficient, but really, it's not. Just because we hope to connect with these people doesn't mean we'll be able to find them and connect with them. So what criteria will we use to specify?

We start with homes at $1 million, and specifically target $2 million and above. That's our first criteria. The next is that they should have owned that home for at least four years. If they've been in their home that long, they might be thinking about moving. If we were to run this campaign in Facebook, we could segment that specific audience.

Assumptions are important because they help you to better design your message. After you've established your criteria, spend some time defining your assumptions. For our campaign, we're assuming these owners will be high-net-worth individuals. That's important for our campaign, because we'll need to make sure that we have a certain tone and demeanor that makes our audience comfortable with us. We've got to be professional enough that high-net-worth people will look at our professional service in the same light and know that we're competent in what we do. If we were marketing to the hipsters of Austin, we wouldn't talk and dress in the same way that we do for this market.

We're also assuming that the individual is selling their home within the next eighteen months. That affects our tracking—their listing could come quite a while from now. If we're only measuring over the next three months, we'll miss out on the results. Every step of the way, a lack of specificity produces disappointment in our marketing campaigns and our real estate career overall.

DESIGN VALUE

What are you offering, not just in your messaging, but as the ultimate offer that the campaign is going to produce? We've specified our objectives and identified our audience, but what does that person want to get from us? We've got to think through what they care about—not just generally, but when selling their real estate specifically.

When we put a marketing campaign in the context of value, it moves us off of the cheesy sales messages. Now, we love cheesy sales messages. We'll be the first to put out a "Seven Steps to a Kick-Butt Marketing Campaign" product. They're fun to come up with, and they get attention, but cheesy sales messages need value. We have to provide value in everything we do. We can't discount the value of what's being offered because we haven't taken the time to construct real value.

If the right person doesn't care about what we're offering, the message will fall on deaf ears. Fifty years of cumulative real estate experience is valuable to a certain person, but if our right person doesn't care about it, there's no value. We've got to extract the value that they will appreciate rather than hoping they'll read between the lines.

Back to the campaign we're building: This value might be a little controversial. You might be surprised or struggle to believe we're even doing it. We know. But we had to try it! We're testing, remember? Usually Garry stops this sort of thing, but we've been talking about it for months, so it's time to test it.

The value we're testing in this campaign for that ultra-high-end customer is a low-cost, flat listing fee. As we've engaged with this kind of customer, we've realized we don't have to do a percentage to offer a great service for them and still make a profit. Now, we're not certain this will make a profit, which is why we've got to test it. But we're sure that there's value *that they will care about.* Instead of paying high commissions, they're going to save money while getting the same level of sophisticated marketing they'd get from anyone else—even more—without high fees.

Don't devalue yourself to offer value to the customer. That won't keep your business afloat. But if you do the math on a $4 million listing, is there that much cost difference between that and a $2 million listing outside of the time frame that it will take to sell that home? We'll do the brochures, drone footage, lifestyle video—nothing will be added to the higher value homes, except we might have to service it longer while we wait for a buyer. We think there is potential in offering an enticing value to the customer without losing anything per listing on our side of the deal. And we're testing it to see whether we're right. At that value, it's worth trying.

Again, this isn't a suggestion for you to mimic. We're simply showing you the process in building and testing a campaign. Design your own value as you come up with your own marketing campaign.

CRAFT THE MESSAGE

When you understand the value and have designed it into your offer, it's time to craft the message. The first step is to create a hook or headline that will get your audience's attention. When you're crafting your marketing message, remember that 90 percent of people will read the headline, but only 10 percent will read the message.

An old marketing trick is to write fifty versions of every headline you make in order to find the right one. That's a bit excessive for what we're doing here, but ten or fifteen wouldn't be a bad idea. If a professional copywriter says it takes dozens of headlines, that means my first headline is probably terrible. We often stop at that first one, so keep writing.

A lot of campaigns lose their intended audiences when we don't give attention to the headline, and because we outsource some of that work. We've found that unless we force our writers to create more than one version of headlines for copy and digital marketing, they won't do it. Digital marketing makes this not only important but also rewarding, because we can vet those different headlines quickly to see what works.

As you craft your message, make sure that the value you've designed is clearly communicated and that your message comes from a specific tone. For our flat-fee offer, our personalized message would need to convey a specific savings amount when hiring our firm, coming from Garry Creath, luxury home sales expert. The tone would be personal yet professional, and the copy might include something like, "If you sold your home for $3.5 million, you would save $55,475 when you work with us."

CREATE A CALL TO ACTION

After it's read the headline, the audience needs to be driven to action. The missing ingredient is usually a sense of urgency. Without that urgency, audience members can read it, be interested, but think they can get around to it later—and they never do.

For our campaign, our call to action is to get our audience to call us: "Call or text Garry at 512-555-5555." For that to happen, we need them to have a reason to care. If they intend to sell, they are likely curious about value and speculating about what needs to happen to get ready to sell, and we can build that into our call to action: "Schedule a consultation to get an analysis of your home's market potential."

But we also need some urgency in order to encourage that call to action, so we'll add "...before you spend money on upgrades or enhancements." Often, when Garry is talking to homeowners, especially in this category, they're thinking about making a significant number of changes because they feel like their home is outdated. In reality, a lot of that money is wasted because they won't recoup it at resale and it won't make their property any more attractive on the market. So the urgency is to catch them before that expense. No one wants to waste money on projects that won't have a return on investment.

DETERMINE DELIVERY

There's a number of ways to get your marketing message out: blog posts, video, an email to networks, a Facebook ad, a phone call—the possibilities are nearly limitless. As you build your campaign, work through the options and decide what media might be best to use or test.

For our campaign, we're going to step back to print marketing, which is still a viable option. We're going to test a mailer once per month for six months, though we might press it to a shorter time frame depending on testing.

What frequency of communication will you use, and when will it take place?

Because there are so many possibilities, feel free to use more than one, which can help with delivery and testing alike. Ask yourself how the message will differ among the media, frequencies, and methods for delivery. For ours, each printed mailer will focus on a different part of the process—one on the person's expenses, another on advanced marketing, and another on preventing an expired listing. Put the same level of care and planning into each and every message that you send, no matter the medium.

WRAP UP THE PLAN

This is where it gets difficult for a lot of people. It's hard to put an idea into action. But we're going to break this step down just like the others to make it feasible. The first questions to ask yourself are simply these: what needs to be created, and what are your deadlines?

Our test campaign will need personalized letters on a letterhead. We'll need printed copies of our property marketing plan. We'll need printed copies of expired listings and sales histories near each home. And when we add phone follow-ups, we'll need a phone script.

When you know the materials necessary for your campaign, decide what needs to be designed. For this campaign, we'd need to feature a Google Street View image of each home within the property marketing plan in order to make a highly personalized mailer.

> In the resources section of our website (www.BlueprintBook. Online), you'll find the template for this same campaign builder so that you can get in the habit of working through these elements as you build your own campaigns.

Finally, what tech support do you need to support your campaign? Ours would likely need a service like REDX to access phone numbers for the follow-up calls. It's a service that we already have, but that's important to know going in.

All of the elements start coming together after we've executed this planning step. The printout with the MLS sheet of expired listings can come with a note using our copy from earlier: "If you sold your home for $3.5 million, you could save $55,475 when you work with us," signed by Garry.

The personalized letter can profile a home that went to market and sold and one that didn't, and then an analysis of what created those outcomes. We can walk through a personal story of homeowners that made different decisions and why working with us created the better outcome, connected with a personalized property marketing plan.

MARKETING CAMPAIGN BUILDER

ACTIVITY	CHECKLIST	RESPONSE [EXAMPLE]
Set Goals or Objectives	What are the campaign's objectives?	*Acquire ultra-high-end listings in our local market.*
		Increase the quantity of conversations we are having with owners of ultra-high-end listings.
	What units of measurement will you use to gauge progress on the objectives?	*# of listings acquired*
		# of listing appointments
		# of initial consultations
		# of conversations initiated
	What criteria are you using to determine if the campaign is a success?	*# of listings acquired*
		# of conversations initiated
	What do you want to learn from this campaign?	*What offer of value will get high-end owners' attention?*
		What sequence of information will provoke a response?
Specify Audience	Who is the target audience for the campaign? What criteria are you using to specify your audience for this campaign?	*Owners of Austin homes worth over $1M.*
		Have owned home for at least 4 years.
	What assumptions are you making about the target audience?	*Owner is a high net-worth individual.*
		Owner lives in home.
		Interested in selling their home in the next 18 months.
Design Value	What value is being offered through this campaign?	*Sophisticated marketing.*
		Detailed project management.
	Why will the target audience care about the value being offered?	*Their homes have higher values, which equate to higher fees. We offer high-level service at a reasonable rate.*

ACTIVITY	CHECKLIST	RESPONSE [EXAMPLE]
Craft Message	What is the message's hook or headline to get the audience's attention?	Personalized message with specific home value and savings represented: "If you sold your home for $3.5 M, you could save $55,475 when you work with Creath Partners."
	How is value being offered through the message?	Specific savings amount when hiring our firm to sell their home.
	Who and what tone should your message come from?	Garry Creath, Luxury Home Sales Expert. Personal yet still professional tone.
Create Call to Action	What is the call to action? Why should the target audience care about or pay attention to it?	Call or text Garry at 512-555-5555 to schedule a consultation to get an analysis of your home's market potential before you spend money on upgrades or enhancements.
	What kind of urgency is included in the message to encourage the call to action?	"Before you spend money on upgrades or enhancements" because they don't want to waste money on projects that won't ROI.
Determine Delivery	What message, media, and medium are being used?	Printed, personalized letter on letterhead. Printed copy of property marketing plan. Printed copy of expired listing near their home's listing history. Phone calls (if number available).
	What is the frequency of communication and when will it take place?	1x per month for 6 months.

ACTIVITY	CHECKLIST	RESPONSE [EXAMPLE]
	What methods of delivery are being used to communicate your messages to the target audience?	*Print and phone.*
	How will the messages differ between the medium, frequencies, and methods of delivery?	*Each printed piece will feature a different part of the total value proposition: savings with competitive, advanced marketing, and preventing expired listing from happening (with emphasis on chasing price).*
Planning	What needs to be created? Deadlines?	*Printed, personalized letters on letterhead.*
		Printed copies of property marketing plan.
		Printed copies of expired listings near their home's listing history.
		Phone script
	What needs to be designed? Deadlines?	*Property marketing plan featuring a Google Street View image of their home.*
	What tech support do you need? Deadlines?	*Possibly using service like REDX for phone numbers.*

KEEP DIGGING

Napoleon Hill's gold miners are all too common in the context of marketing. It really doesn't matter what kind of marketing activity we're talking about; the most common experience is simply giving up too early. We're still guilty of it. You get into some type of new marketing activity and your first results come up empty or even bad, so you throw up your hands. You quit digging. You decide it's not for you, and you move on.

This Facebook thing doesn't work for me. These Google ads don't work for my business. LinkedIn isn't for me. Social media doesn't do anything for my business. Websites don't work for what I do.

Less than 4 percent of real estate business comes through a real estate website. Why? Because those agents believe a website isn't going to do anything for them. They haven't committed to learning the skill necessary to be successful with that marketing piece. So they give up too early—even though they could be just steps away from a breakthrough. It's much easier to blame technology or to just roll with the ebb and flow of the market than to commit to developing new skills. But if there's a small percentage of people who are having success with a marketing tool or technology, you simply are not doing it right.

Push through. Keep digging. Acquire that skill—whether that means getting an education, putting money into it to test it, or working with someone else. Do what you need to do to take those steps toward a breakthrough. And give the results time to show up. Remember that what you do today won't show benefits for about ninety days. If you do things today and then give up tomorrow, you'll never see the results.

If you don't use your tried-and-true templates for initial consultations or listing presentations, no matter how many times you do it, you're likely to miss something. The same goes for marketing. The problem is that when you miss something in marketing, you pay the price later. You pay in taking longer to get the campaign in place. You pay in lost opportunity and money wasted.

In a ninety-day real estate cycle, it's tempting to do the marketing and prospecting that brings you clients but then stop marketing because you're busy. What's going to happen ninety days after you stop marketing? Nothing. So the scramble starts up all over again, earning real estate its reputation for being feast or famine. The truth is that success in this business is a matter of consistent effort in effective measures.

Use these resources that we've tested for you and have seen succeed time and again so that your own resources—time, money, and energy—can go straight into your business. Don't forget that it can all apply to any form of marketing—not just large campaigns, but something as small as a one-off postcard or personal note. When you're thinking about the right person with the right message at the right time, and designing value and crafting messages that they will appreciate, there's a good chance they'll hear you, gain interest, and take action.

SOMETHING TO THINK ABOUT

Think back over the last ninety days. Have your marketing efforts been sufficient to keep new business at your door? Is your ninety-day cycle about to collapse again? What can you do today to jumpstart your business ninety days from now?

8

FINANCES

Stop right there—don't put the book down. We know finances aren't sexy. We know you're probably number averse. We know you've been putting off looking at your finances. If we're honest, there are some things in life that we're inclined to ignore. The door in the hallway that "sticks." That one tooth that hurts now and then. The mole that looks a little suspicious. The bank account balance.

At least for a little while, it feels like we're getting away with ignoring the little things. But then that door that sticks might turn into a cracked wall. And then those cracks might get bigger. The longer we ignore the growing signs of trouble, the bigger the consequences will be. Walls don't just crack. Teeth don't just ache. There's always something more going on, and finances are no different. They are the foundation of your business, and if you don't pay attention to the little signs and signals of trouble, eventually those problems will get bigger and bigger until eventually the foundation completely fails and it all comes crashing in.

The thing is, for many of us, something has already collapsed to get us to this point in the first place. What twelve-year-old kid says, "I want to be a *broker* when I grow up"? Most of us started out somewhere else and then wound up here when life took unexpected turns, careers ended, or we just needed something different from life than what we were getting. In other words, we were using other blueprints to build different lives. We hadn't tailored our education and life experience to be able to seamlessly step into running a successful real estate business.

In fact, of all of the professional backgrounds out there, more than 80 percent of people in real estate came from a background *other than* management, business, or finance. Not only did we not set our lives up for real estate, but most of us also didn't even set out to build or manage a business at all. If you're cringing at this chapter title and feeling like you just don't have the skills or tools you need to get your finances in order, don't worry. You're in the good company of the vast majority of real estate professionals.

Not surprisingly, most real estate agents don't even separate their business and personal finances at all—money goes into their checking account and back out and it's all mixed in with their household expenses, just like it was in their previous job. Except for those 19 percent or so who have a background in this stuff, most of us struggle through periods of feast and famine until we reach a measure of success via the school of hard knocks or intentional education.

We know we want to sell real estate and we often find ourselves leading a team, but we lack the framework and skills to track, assess, and plan finances on any sort of scale. Budgeting, reconciliation, and financing terms and tasks seem to come in a foreign language. Unfortunately for us all, however, finance is the foundation of business, and ignoring it can lead to critical issues. Without a handle on finance, it's impossible to know where to apply your focus, make investments, pull back on expenses, or make any sort of adjustment to grow your business.

We can relate, because we've been there (Chris has, for sure—Garry is more inclined to be the money guy). We've seen how quickly a foundation can fail, and we want you to catch those creaks and cracks before they grow into a bigger problem. We want to see your business built on a solid foundation. In this chapter and in the coaching work that we do, we want to give you the tools you'll need to focus on your foundation and to operate and grow your business with sound financials.

ORGANIZE AND REVIEW YOUR DATA REGULARLY

When we fall into real estate without a background in finance or someone to help hold us accountable, a lot of bad habits can form. Not looking at your accounts at all is one of the simplest habits to correct, to great impact, as we'll look at more closely in a minute. But that's not the worst of them. What's far more dangerous and far too common is when you never open those accounts in the first place.

Too many Realtors® never open a separate checking account or credit card for their business, so all of their income and expenses flow through their home accounts. Everything becomes comingled and muddled together. Where is that money going? Well, some is going to rent and some to groceries. It's certainly not going to go into business development. Why? Because it's impossible to manage your business money when you treat it like grocery money.

If you're going to run a business, you have to treat it *like a business*. You can't expect to have $10 million in sales when you treat your business like a side endeavor.

You can't track your numbers well—or at all—if you don't

have separate accounts set up. And if you're not tracking your numbers, how in the world will you know what to do next? How will you know whether you can spend another thousand dollars on Facebook or whether you need to get rid of a monthly expense that you're not using? You might have a sense of what you're doing, but you'll never know exactly how it's going.

After you have separate bank and credit card accounts set up, you have to look at them. If you put everything on a designated credit card, you have to reconcile that account. If you don't, things will get out of control. Every month, maybe even a couple of times a month, you've got to look at your accounts to see what's happening. Look at where your money came from. Notice where the money was spent. Note where your business came from. Decide whether business is going up, going down, or staying the same. Decide the same for expenses. Then ask yourself how you can make those numbers better. You have to experience the emotions that come with disappointing numbers so that you have the drive to turn them into positive numbers.

Just the simple act of looking at the numbers and noticing trends can give you a basic handle on finances, enough to make a massive impact on your business. You'll see things pop up that you no longer use, and need to get rid of. You'll see where your business came from, and patterns can signal a market to pursue more intentionally. All of these growth points start to come together—but not until you look at the numbers.

LEVERAGE OTHER PEOPLE'S EXPERIENCE

Finance is so critical to your business that we could spend far too much time talking about it, but don't worry. We won't. There are people who spend years studying finance, and we call them CPAs—certainly not real estate professionals. These are your true financial experts, and we highly recommend you work with them. Most of you will hire someone to do your bookkeeping. That's good. Some of you will balk at the idea.

We usually categorize roles as one of three functions: revenue production, expense production, and profit production. When you think of the finance side of an organization—be honest—where do you think they fall? Definitely expense production, right? They're an empty cost that doesn't provide direct return? Well, not necessarily. They might not be generating revenue by making sales or closing deals, but anyone keeping your finances in check can be a profit producer. They have a critical relationship to the bottom line, which gives them a critical role in profit production. Only the person in financials can really direct you toward how much needs to be created or spent to meet that bottom line.

Hiring an expert doesn't mean letting go of your finances entirely. After you do turn your bookkeeping and tracking over to an accountant or virtual assistant, you need to know how to evaluate the information they'll report and how to ask the right questions to turn the data into action and improve your business.

One of the biggest mistakes that we've made in business has been to abdicate financials to an expert. Take note of that carefully chosen word there, *abdicate*. We don't mean that it was a mistake to hire help. Dictionary.com is brutal in its definition: "to fail to fulfill or undertake (a responsibility or duty)."

The pitfall here is that hiring a bookkeeper is delegation, not abdication. There's a key distinction here. Everyone should eventually be able to delegate their bookkeeping. But that doesn't mean the bookkeeper is then responsible for the financials and you are free to ignore it. Like the foundation of a house, we have to be constantly aware that the financials are solid, or whether we need to take action to address something before it gets out of hand.

It's painful to look at your finances on a regular basis. All of those questions linger: What am I going to find? Do I really want to know? Discomfort aside, we've got to get it done. Garry likes to do a quick review of the financials weekly, while Chris takes a look every month. The more time goes by in between reviewing the financials, the more apprehension builds up around it. Incidentally, though there usually aren't as many bad things lurking as we imagine there will be, the more time that goes by in between reviews, the higher the likelihood that something is getting worse.

Ignoring it won't make it better, any more than ignoring your waistline will make pizza and hot dogs a good choice for lunch every day. Or ignoring skin cancer will make it go away. Or letting those cracks grow will keep your house on solid ground.

You might never, personally, go any deeper into finance than simply looking at the numbers and asking the right questions. We'll look a little bit at some documentation that can help you improve your financials, but what you really need to learn is how to ask the right questions. How can you dig down to the information that will help you improve profitability?

ASK THE RIGHT QUESTIONS

In any review of financial information, you're tracking changes: what increased, what decreased, and what stayed the same. Those trends are going to pop out at you, especially if your bookkeeper or technology is turning the hard numbers into reports and charts for you. So the first and main question you need to ask is simply, "Why?"

Why is the margin where it is? Why are my expenses what they are? Why is that number going up? Noticing is a good start, but it's not going to be enough for long. You might notice that your expenses have gone down, and on the surface that can seem like a good thing. But if you need more business and you're spending less on marketing, that number probably needs to be going up instead of down.

Noticing that your income has gone up is great, but is that because you're not taking adequate compensation? A 10 percent margin looks great for your business, sure. Not so much if you're following Gwyneth Paltrow's "intentional" food stamp diet to get by. That's not exactly success.

Even if everything looks great, if you don't look deeper and ask why, how will you be able to duplicate that success? How will you be able to stop it from reversing? If you know why, you'll know how to make better quality decisions and get better results. You'll start to be in control of the changes.

TECHNOLOGY THAT MAKES FINANCE QUICK AND (MOSTLY) PAINLESS

Although finance never changes, the tools and technologies we use to track them are constantly changing. The good news is that today's tools make finances easy and quick. The bad news is there's a lot to choose from.

When you're going to prepare a meal, if you want a quality dinner, you'll need quality ingredients. Canned sides will bring an entire meal down, no matter how good the food that it's paired with. The quality that goes in is the quality that will come out. So when we find ourselves without the right financial information (or structure, or tools, or vendors), we have to consider what quality went into it in the first place.

EXCEL

There are some portals that just give bad data. They come up with wild and inaccurate estimates because they're putting in the wrong data and bad data's coming out. When you start tracking your accounts and activity, be meticulous about it. The right categories and labeling are your ingredients. You wouldn't put frozen fish with a steak dinner, so don't cut corners here, either. Build a solid structure, and then put good data into it.

We're going to start simple, with an Excel spreadsheet for you to manage your finances from. This is going to become your chart of accounts, which is a list of everything that brings income in or takes expenses out. It doesn't have to be elaborate or fancy. Just input every applicable account, and label them. With everything added, your chart of accounts becomes a categorization tool for you to label everything coming in and going out of the business.

QUICKBOOKS

Depending on what version you have, QuickBooks can come in several different platforms. Most people use the mobile app, but a lot of us still have it on our desktops. We like QuickBooks Online, which you can download to your desktop. This way, you have all of the updated features of the website with the convenience of desktop access.

You can create a chart of accounts in QuickBooks just like you can in Excel—it just might look a little bit different. The point is that you can try different technologies until you find one that's designed for what you actually need. Quicken, for example, is a popular financial app, but it's built for personal use rather than business transactions.

EVERNOTE

Real estate is a highly litigious industry. Really, we have a litigious culture. We've lost count of the times we've had to get on a phone call with the Texas Workforce Commission over various issues. Every time, documentation has been our saving grace.

We have folders in Evernote for every financial and HR action. Resumes from every interview, notes from every review, and all of our onboarding documentation for employees and contractors go into their own files and folders. Tax returns, income statements, bank statements, receipts, chart of accounts—all financial documentation goes into its own files and folders as well.

If you ever wind up audited, in front of a board for something, in a litigation situation, or even just applying for a loan, Evernote or another kind of organizational, cloud-based structure will make it so much less stressful. Just share the folder or file that contains the information you need.

GOOD FINANCE TRACKING CREATES GOOD PACING

No matter who you hire or work with, you're almost certainly going to be the CFO of your business. The buck stops here. A bookkeeper is responsible for making sure the data goes in, and can report, project, and even request funding where necessary. But it's up to the CFO—it's up to you—to decide what those categories are going to be. Your bookkeeper can track everything for you, but you've still got to look through it at a granular level so that you can make the right decisions.

In our company, we set up a budget for the whole year during an annual meeting. We look at the previous year and the year to come and lay out goals and clear financial objectives. But things change. At the beginning of 2007, we had certain goals and objectives. Then the market crashed—hard. If we hadn't changed everything, we would have set ourselves up for massive failure. Another time, we cleaned house and hired completely new agents. We had to pivot and adjust.

If you had a goal of running a marathon with a nine-minute-mile pace, but you weren't allowed a watch, could you hit that target? Not a chance. Think of your budget as that nine-minute mile and your records as the watch. Organizing it all is a preemptive step—it's mapping out your training course. It's a good start. And we like good starts. We follow the philosophy of the great Bill Murray: baby steps.

After you've mapped it for a couple of months in a row, you can start to set bigger goals. Start to review your documents with an accountability partner. It could be someone within the business, a coach, or an accountant. This step helps you dig a bit further. When Chris first started managing businesses, he could look at financials whenever he needed to, but he didn't understand them. He couldn't harness the power behind solid financials until he'd done it for a long time.

When you look at them with someone with experience or with that education to know what they're talking about, you skip those years of growing pains and benefit from their perspective and expertise.

One pass through the data can get you organized and get everything where it needs to be. There are only so many real estate deals over the course of a month, so you can relatively easily see whether everything is where it needs to be. Then, on another look at the numbers, you'll start to notice where unnecessary costs are happening. Maybe you're paying for an operational task that you don't even use. Then later, you'll be able to look at the data even more closely to spot growth opportunities. This is where you can start to forecast—will you need to reserve some for an impending downturn, or can you invest and take advantage of a potential opportunity?

A BETTER MEASURE OF SUCCESS

We acknowledge that even the promise of control is not enough to make finances sexy. It's still not a fun thing to participate in. So let's reframe it a bit. Instead of looking at finances as fun, and instead of looking at them as a discipline, think of the possibilities. Instead of thinking about the finance tasks ahead, think about it in these terms:

What new results can I produce? What new future can I create for myself, my family, and my business? What possibilities are waiting for me behind this review, from where we are, in what we're tracking? How can we open ourselves up to that future?

Finance as a practice is rooted in the future. You see where you've been, forecast where you're going, and take action to make that future potential even brighter. You're going to start predicting how much money you're going to make—which is always nice for people who like to have food with their dinnertime. You're going to be able to see investments and loss coming so that you can prepare for either, making sound investments—not just in the stock market or property, but in your company, your personnel, and your culture.

When you handle them well, finances are a blueprint in and of themselves. They're the most accurate measure of success—am I building what I intended to build?—than anything else. The egregious error that we see people making in the real estate industry is that they are measuring their success based on sales production. They hold up $X million in real estate sales as an accomplishment or standard or goal. They win awards based on their sales volume. They brag about their millions sold. It can sound impressive, sure. That's great.

But we don't give a shit about any of that. We truly could not care less. What we care about is what's in the bank.

Remember how Garry looked up to that agent who was selling $50 million back when he was still growing his business? He'd gone to his mentor with stars in his eyes, sure that if he was taking home six figures at the sales volume he was carrying, that this woman was taking home a million dollars a year. Dee's advice was simply, "You're looking at the wrong metric."

We can promote and advertise and spend ourselves into the red. At the end of the day, what really matters is how solid the foundation is. Sales volume is fun and exciting, and sexy to track. But it doesn't tell you much at all about the stability and strength of your business. Take the time to track the right metric—become familiar with your finances, catch little things before they grow to big collapses, and start to celebrate and applaud the right kind of success.

Speaking of which—applaud yourself for making it through a chapter on finances. In the next chapter, with a solid financial foundation that supports strong sales and marketing and client interactions, you can start to substantiate those big goals you've set for yourself.

SOMETHING TO THINK ABOUT

When was the last time you looked at your financials? Identify where you fall on the financial health spectrum—from holding all of your finances in the same account to having a bookkeeper to never looking at the numbers to always evaluating your circumstances. What steps can you take this month to improve your financials and firm up your foundation?

9

SUBSTANTIATED BUSINESS PLANNING

Now that you've survived the chapter on finance—because we know you didn't just skip it, *right?*—let's wake you up with a shock:

Most people don't achieve the goals that they've set.

Okay, you're not surprised at all. A study in 2007 tracked 3,000 people who set goals like losing weight, making more money, or stopping a bad habit. At the beginning of the study, a slight majority of the participants felt confident in reaching their goals. But by the end, only

12 percent had made it happen.* Let's rephrase that for some perspective: almost nine out of ten participants failed to reach their goals.

They almost certainly failed because they didn't make a plan for how to get there. In the absence of a plan, we're just hoping that we can think about our goals enough to make them happen.

The entrepreneur does something that the real estate agent often misses. An entrepreneur knows that you can break your long-term goals down into a set of daily activities that, if you successfully complete them each day, will ensure you hit those long-term targets. If you want to hit your sales goals, you need a blueprint to get there. If you don't dive into enough detail to understand exactly what you want and what it's going to take to get there, you will fall behind and ultimately give up.

WHY HUSTLE FAILS

In 1997, when the internet was still a feature for universities and the government, the MLS transitioned from printed books to an online database. Garry started real estate around that time as part of a large firm where his parents had been housing their license. He walked into

---

* Richard Wiseman, "New Year's Resolution Project." Accessed January 2019. http://www.richardwiseman.com/quirkology/new/USA/Experiment_resolution.shtml

the luxury division of the company, where the office manager walked him to a room and said, "Here's your desk. There's your phone, and..." *plop*. A giant phone book for the city of Austin. "...here's your list of clients. Get busy."

That was it. That's how Garry picked up foundational real estate. The prevailing school of thought was that real estate was a numbers game. Call as many people as possible using the exact same script for them all, and eventually you'll get an appointment. It wasn't about the connection or marketing or anything else at all. It was just about the numbers and the hustle.

Those habits are hard to break. Think about goals you've set recently or in the past. You probably had a clear, if distant, target in mind. You could see yourself at the finish line, and you were excited and driven to get there. You had motivational coaching clichés in your ear, and you were ready to hustle until your dreams came true.

Because you're reading this book, it's probably a safe assumption that you didn't make it to that goal. Why? You cannot create a 500 percent increase or achieve any sort of lofty goal on pure hustle.

There is a terrible breakdown in the industry at this point in particular. People create goals around hopeful, overly optimistic intentions, and then of course they are going to fail. Trying harder gets you through a few days or weeks, but it doesn't take long to start to question the effort and even the goal. Setting intention isn't granular enough. There's not enough human volition to carry you through an intention that hasn't been substantiated.

It becomes a cycle of starting the year with hope, getting lost in the grind, ending the year depressed, and then starting it all over again, determined to try harder.

Trying harder isn't going to get you to your goals. You have to actually do things differently than you've done them in the past. You have to substantiate the numbers you want to hit. You might have to hire assistants, spend money on marketing, and buy some tools to offset it all. You can't grit your teeth through a goal. You've got to connect the dots, realize what you can do, and then find the support mechanisms you can invest in to realize that goal.

WHY WE FAIL

There's a limit to what your body can do. There's a limit to the number of hours you can work. The older we all get, the less we can do. Instead of deciding to just work more hours, what we work on is reducing the sales cycle. We have to cut down on the amount of time we spend generating, converting, and selling leads. We have to increase sales price, reduce the sales cycle, and MAYBE increase the number of transactions. That's been our goal with our courses and this book—you shouldn't have to keep running around ragged doing the same thing you did last year, hoping for a different outcome.

The University of Maryland and University of Toronto collaborated on a study that shifted goal-setting theory to identify reasons people don't succeed.* Even if you have a clear goal, if your map isn't detailed enough, you're not going to get there. If you want to go from Austin to Denver and just plan to sort of go northwest, you won't make it. If you want to convert body weight to muscle but don't have a plan or someone holding you accountable, it won't happen. These are the obstacles that they've found keep us from attaining our goals, plus another that we've found to be true in real estate specifically.

The first hang-up is that we're simply not committed. This can happen even when you start with good intentions and hustle. Say your goal is to add one hundred deals this year. Great. Do you know what it is you have to do to make that happen? More deals mean more contacts and more outreach. When you find out you have to make 300 phone calls a day, you might lose that commitment.

---

* Gary Latham and Edwin Locke, 2007. "New Developments in and Directions for Goal-Setting Research," University of Toronto. Accessed http://www-2.rotman. utoronto.ca/facbios/file/28%20-%20Latham%20&%20Locke%20Euro%20 Psych%202007.pdf

Another reason people don't succeed—and one we often don't want to admit—is that we simply cannot do it. If you're a buyer's agent with a goal of becoming a listing agent and selling fifty properties in a year, you probably don't have the skills yet. You have to acknowledge your limitations and do what's needed to overcome them in order to meet your goals. You don't need a better mindset in this instance—you need different knowledge and better tools.

The third reason the study noted as a reason we don't meet our goals is that we don't realize our goals conflict. A lofty goal for business might require being in the office sixteen hours a day. But if you also have goals of being physically fit or coaching your son's soccer team, there are inherent conflicts in your goals. Those conflicts will prevent you from moving forward. And a lot of times, instead of reassessing to compromise and make changes, we just give up.

We'll add another obstacle here, and it's one that is especially pervasive in real estate: you're simply doing the wrong things. You can "hustle" for twenty-three hours a day and catnap in between, but if you're doing the wrong activities in the first place, you won't get ahead.

For example, you might start with the assumption that connecting with people on social media will help. But that's a false assumption. So even if you spend all of your time connecting with people on social media and commenting on posts, you won't sell any more homes. That's not selling; that's stalking. Forget what anyone has told you about doing that more. Do that less. People don't want that.

Peter Drucker had it right: "there is nothing so useless as doing efficiently that which should not be done at all." We can organize, structure, and work hard at something that's still not the right thing to do. Efficiency is not enough. We want effectiveness—doing the *right* thing well.

Unsubstantiated efforts are distractions. We place our hopes on these solutions that don't actually solve anything, and no matter how much we hope we're not wasting our time, we're not actually getting any more business.

SUBSTANTIATE YOUR GOALS

When we set goals for ourselves and our agents in our firm, we make sure we can back it up with specific activities. If you don't have a goal, we start by identifying your target number—how much you need to earn in a year to live your best life now and to prepare for and invest in the future. Every month, we forecast revenue with a certain percentage of error. If it's not going to be enough to hit that number, it's time to kick into gear.

For every goal, we make a detailed plan that takes all of those limiting factors into account. We do this by backing into the goal with a specific planning process. What are you going to do differently? What points of value can you implement? What marketing will you do? What prospecting activities will you do? What has to take place to get you from point A to point B? Wanting means nothing without the details in place.

If you want to sell $10 million in real estate, how many contracts will it take to make that happen? To get those contracts, you'll need a certain number of appointments. To get those appointments, you'll need to do a certain number of activities.

This becomes a simple mathematical analysis that anyone can do. Start with your overall goal and then break it down, step by step, until you've identified specific activities that you need to do X number of times each week in order to substantiate the goal you've set for yourself over the year.

When you know what you're supposed to do in order to substantiate your goals, your activity has to reflect it. Your day-to-day life has to be what substantiates that goal. Your calendar will show you how you're spending your time and whether your level of commitment matches your ambition. If it doesn't, don't give up. Reassess, resubstantiate, and keep moving forward until your blueprint becomes reality.

CONCLUSION

Garry fell into real estate when his father suddenly passed away. He was trained up in the old-school hustle mentality, and he broke through it to create a better structure for his business alongside Chris, who brought his own varied strengths and experience to the table. You've read through the book with us as we shared our weaknesses and lived experience, and we've given you the blueprints you need to hopefully bypass many of the struggles we've overcome.

But it's in the gaps and spaces where the story really lies. When Garry was still in Colorado, he was working at a ski resort because he was a medic. That's where his training was. So when he got the call that his dad had died, the first thing he wanted to do was question the fire department. Volunteers had responded to the 911 call, and Garry wanted to know exactly what they did to help and why the outcome had been so tragic. *Could anything have been done differently? Better?*

As soon as he got back in town, Garry drove right to the fire department and asked to speak with the chief.

"This is what happened," he told them, recounting the story and the volunteers that he'd spoken with. "I need to thank the chief." He invited Chief Paul Barker—a kind, gentle soul and friend to this day—and the entire department over for a dinner. Garry understood that, when someone is kind to you or offers you something of value, you turn it around to ask, "What can I do to help?" Each person at his table that day and with his dad weeks before had been a volunteer, simply helping out from the kindness of their hearts. And they needed more volunteers.

For the next ten years, Garry reciprocated that value by helping their volunteer fire department. His training served him well, and the chief was serious about the department being stretched thin. Garry was on call almost every day for a decade—the same decade in which he was building his real estate business from a phone book. He'd drive to the office in the rescue truck and a uniform and then make his prospecting calls until tones dropped and he was dispatched. After the call, he'd get back in the truck and go straight back to the office—no A/C, no strategy, no light at the end of the tunnel.

In the beginning, Garry was new to the area and didn't have friends, a girlfriend, or other distractions to slow his pace. Over the years, he did pick up some specific practices to make it more sustainable, and more technology did come out to make it more feasible. But, as we said in chapter 9, the human body can only take so much.

The adrenaline spikes and crashes that came from the emergency calls, and the exhaustion that came from never slowing down, completely burned through Garry's adrenals. One day, when the third phone that week broke from Garry slamming them down in anger and frustration, his mentor and manager came in to say, "I need your phone. You're going on vacation." This happened every six to nine months, for four or five years. A constant cycling of hustle, burnout, and trying again.

There aren't enough pages to walk you through everything Garry learned from those experiences. There's not enough time to relay everything Chris has learned in marketing that has so aptly applied to real estate. And there's so much potential ahead of you that can come from these practices. But it's in all of the spaces between the practices and prescriptions that we've offered throughout the book—asking questions, reciprocating value, substantiating a sustainable business—that we find that human element. The stories that taught us, shaped us, and connect us.

The real estate industry is severely lacking in support for its professionals, and it takes a lot to overcome the bad habits formed from well-meaning advice. Our goal in this book has been to give you a solid survey of tools, mindset, and habits that can give you a better outcome, without the burnout.

Keep this book on hand. As you take small steps forward—reviewing your financials, assessing and substantiating your goals, creating points of value—come back to review the book. What steps can you take next? If you keep working on your business and keep spending time on these small steps, you'll have what you need to carry you into the future. This isn't something you can digest in one sitting, apply all at once, and suddenly hit that $10 million goal. This is just the beginning of the change.

It's going to take weeks, months, sometimes even years for you to be able to take your new knowledge and skills and make them part of who you are—part of your regular practice. It's okay if it's months before you're regularly reviewing your financials. It's okay if it takes time to stick to the daily activities you need to do to meet your goals. All good things take time to produce. And you need to grant yourself some grace.

In the process of review and reflection, prioritize your time. Which tools or skills need more of your attention?

What will open up possibilities for you to produce a better outcome? Which chapters were a struggle for you, where you might need to spend more time revisiting and getting a better grasp on them? Spend time reflecting on your own practice and performance to better prioritize your next steps.

If you aren't sure where to begin, go back to the earlier chapters and look at those points of value. What can you identify as an opportunity within your business? Now set a goal—a specific goal with a deadline—to implement that point of value. When you can produce new possibilities, you're opening up a new future for yourself, your family, and your business. Those small changes lead to another, and then another. Eventually you'll notice that you're growing and you've built some momentum. A month or two goes by, and then a year, and at some point you'll turn around and realize that you're not just an agent or an employee anymore—you're a business owner. You're not burned out and running ragged anymore. You're thinking from an entirely different perspective.

Ultimately, that moment of change happens when you make the choice to apply something you've learned.

That moment doesn't have to happen immediately. It can be wise to take a little bit of a break and sit with what you're learning and where your business stands. You've absorbed a lot and worked on a lot. Take some time to think about things that stood out, things that you've learned, and things you want to learn more about in the future. Acknowledge what you do really well, and figure out why that is.

Finally, and most importantly, find a mentor. Identify someone who is performing at a greater level than you are, and look for their help. Tiger Woods always kept a minimum of five coaches—long game, short game, putting, swing, and physical training. In real estate, we're just thrown into the business with the virtual equivalent of a phone book and the command to "Go for it." That just doesn't work anymore.

Find people who have cracked the code and are making it work. Years ago, a coach simply said, "Garry, you're doing great work." When Garry pressed for advice on how to build more business, the coach said, "Do more of what you're doing." Garry fired that coach. More of what we're doing isn't going to change where we are. What we need is to know the next steps. What we need is someone who is researching potential and developing their business.

As individual real estate agents, we can't be our own research and development resources. It's not sustainable. So we have to surround ourselves with people who get it, who are growing, and who will help us take the next steps. That might look like everything from mentorship groups like the ones we host to support from someone in your community to books and resources that successful people from the past have left behind. Some of the mentors who had the greatest influence in our business and our lives had died before we were even born. Mentors don't have to have a direct, one-on-one relationship with you to impact your life and your business. They simply need to have the skills and wisdom to direct you where you need to go.

No matter what your background is or what level of success or struggle your business is at, incredible potential is laid out in front of you. You've got the blueprints—the tools, resources, mindset, and ability—to reach that target number, thrive in your business, and enjoy your career in real estate. It doesn't happen by trying harder. It doesn't happen by doing more. It's about substantiated goals and effective actions, constantly assessed and reassessed until your lifestyle aligns with your ambition and you realize your goals.

As you begin to implement this new thinking and these strategies and practices, remember that you are not alone. We are an enormous industry of loving and caring people who, for the most part, are here to help each other out. Reach out and find the right network of professionals who can help you. Find a mentor.

Get help.

A lot of it.

You're building a business, now. You don't have to go it alone.

ABOUT THE AUTHORS

GARRY CREATH is a quintessential real estate entre-preneur. He has been a top selling agent in Austin, Texas for over twenty-one years, has owned and run his own real estate brokerage with over thirty-five agents, and has been featured by Apple Computers and Evernote in case studies. At the peak of his real estate sales career, Garry was going on six listing appointments per week and was carrying over fifty-five listings at a time. Garry not only represents buyers and sellers in real estate, he also invests in residential and commercial real estate as a part of his retirement portfolio. He is a real estate tech company startup advisor and investor and is constantly on the lookout for ways to build efficiencies that make real estate businesses more profitable for brokers and agents alike. When he's not selling real estate, training agents, or advising business owners, Garry travels and explores the world with his wife, Pamela.

CHRIS SCOTT is a digital and real estate marketing expert at The Paperless Agent, an e-learning company that shows real estate practitioners how to improve their performance with technology and online marketing. Over the course of his career, Chris has been a software developer, product manager specializing in subscription models, has worked with the real estate industry's most well-known leaders, and ran sales and marketing for a two-time Inc. 500 award-winning company. Chris hosts weekly webcasts to an audience of 4,000 real estate professionals every month, manages social media accounts with over 200,000 followers, runs a team that generates over 6,000 leads per month, and manages marketing for their real estate firm in Austin, Texas. When he's not marketing or managing his businesses, you can find Chris spending time with his spouse of over thirteen years and four kids. In addition to family and career, he spends a considerable amount of time reading books on theology, philosophy, and historical fiction.